The PURSUIT of BEAUTY

The

PURSUIT

of

BEAUTY

FINDING CONTENTMENT
WITH THE YOU GOD MADE

New Leaf Press

First printing: March 1998

ISBN: 0-89221-373-6
Library of Congress Number: 97-75890

Cover by Left Coast Design, Portland, OR.

Printed in the United States of America.

Dedication

To Ron Luce, my husband and closest friend. If it weren't for his unconditional love for me I would have never had a book to write. In my darkest times I thought, *If Ron still loves me after all I've done, God **must** love me.* What an example he is! He has truly earned my highest respect and lifelong allegience.

To Myles Munroe, our spiritual daddy, who taught us how to soar.

To my precious, praying mother and grandmother whose faithfulness, love, and courage has been my anchor.

To Laura Koke, my Jonathan/David friend — we've slayed many giants together, and many more to come.

TABLE OF CONTENTS

SECTION 3
TRUE BEAUTY

SECTION 4
THE PREVENTION OF EATING DISORDERS
AND HELPING THOSE WHO HAVE THEM

Foreword

On my way to London, waiting for my flight from New York, I stopped briefly in an airport newsstand to pick up a weekly news magazine. As I stood before the massive rack, plastered with every type of magazine covering every topic imaginable, I was amazed at the number of covers decorated with the face of a well-painted female. I started to count the number, and decided to stop at 25.

It was a shock to me — the preoccupation of our society with the passion for physical beauty. We have heard the stories of the millions of people, especially women, possessed by the spirit of the diet. The explosion of health spas, exercise gymns, and physical development programs is evidence of the craze taking over the average members of our communities.

Many rich, famous, and wealthy tell stories of their pursuit of beauty at the expense of their health and personal safety. The health food industry and cosmetic sales total in the billions of dollars. All of these give evidence of the craving in the human heart for a sense of self-worth, social approval, and a measure of acceptable beauty. However, for many this passion is simply the surfacing of self-hatred, low self-esteem, and shallow self-worth. It is a sign of a defective self-concept.

Katie Luce, in this work titled *The Pursuit of Beauty,*

writes from the weighty perspective of personal experience and addresses this subject with depth, precision, simplicity, and crisp insight. She further provides practical principles designed to give the reader immediate steps for application. This subject is one that has not received much attention, even though it is a common experience among most of us, especially the younger generation. I encourage you to read these pages carefully and embrace the wisdom, knowledge, and understanding hidden there. Your life will never be the same and your measure of value and worth related to personal beauty will be completely transformed as you learn the meaning of true beauty. It will also inspire you to re-order your priorities in life and bring a discipline to your body that expresses the spirit of dignity, peace, and self-confidence. You are beautiful. Let this book help you bring it out.

Dr. Myles Munroe
Nassau, Bahamas

Beauty Is Fleeting

I've wasted many hours of my life, thinking, planning, and dreaming, all in the pursuit of beauty. I think most women do. Television, movies, advertisements, and magazines bombard us daily with the same message. How to be a knockout in ten days or less. Lose that ugly cellulite. Buns of steel. How to look 20 years younger. And all for what? For a great body? For that perfect image? I don't think that's all there is to it — I think we long to be fulfilled in life. To feel better about ourselves. Everyone wants that. Every woman wants to feel beautiful, and ultimately . . . loved.

The problem is, the more we focus on outside beauty, the less fulfillment comes on the inside. I know; I tried it. Bulimia is not a fun road to travel. But many women, in the pursuit of beauty, find themselves on that road or other similar roads, trying to grab hold of something, anything, to help them feel good about themselves. Their lifelong search ends in emptiness, not attaining the self-love and peace they so desperately desire. They never find the beauty God had planned for them specifically, for their search took them in a different direction.

The funny thing is, this thing called beauty that everyone craves doesn't even last long. The Bible says, "Charm is deceitful and beauty is passing" (Prov. 31:30). And it's true! No matter how much cream, oil, scrubs, or masks we put on our face, the inevitable comes . . . wrinkles! Gray hair, sags, bags; it all happens to the best of us sooner or later. So why waste so much brain-space, time, and energy on something that's not eternal?

The verse above goes on to say that "a woman who fears the Lord, she shall be praised." I think that's *God's* definition of true beauty — a woman who fears the Lord. A beautiful woman, in the Lord's eyes, is one who gives her life away for Him. That kind of beauty cannot be bought, isn't a fad, and doesn't fade. It's eternal.

Real beauty is a rare quality that few find because it doesn't come easily or even naturally. It takes much refinement, like gold in the fire, a precisely cut jewel, or a shaped clay pot on the wheel. Only a submitted life can be shaped and molded by the Potter. When we finally give up our own ambitions, our own search for ourselves, He is free to make the heap of once useless clay into a beautiful piece of art — useful, and a joy to everyone, especially the Potter.

True beauty comes from God's love inside our hearts. It gives sparkle to our eyes, joy and shine to our faces, and energy to our bodies. It outlives our wrinkles and gray hair, giving us meaning and purpose. It gives us the ability to truly love ourselves, which empowers us to love others. We can finally take our focus off of ourselves and see this world through the eyes of God.

This is the story of my personal search for the true beauty in myself. What you are about to read are some of the most difficult and painful times of my life. If it were up to me, I would rather have hidden it away, put it behind me, and shown only my strength. But that's not the Lord's way. He shows His glory and strength through our weaknesses.

He said to me . . . my strength is made
perfect in weakness. Therefore I will boast all
the more gladly about my weaknesses, so that
Christ's power may rest on me. . . . For when I
am weak, then I am strong (2 Cor. 12:9-10).

This is a true account of one very weak and desperate person finding herself, hidden in Christ. I never would
have written a book if I hadn't seen these same truths
work so successfully time after time in others with similar struggles. I pray that you will be encouraged by the
truth found within these pages. I also pray that you will
become the real you, the incredibly beautiful you, that
God created you to be.

The Spirit of the Sovereign Lord is on me,
(Jesus) . . . to bestow on them a crown of beauty
instead of ashes, the oil of gladness instead of
mourning, and a garment of praise instead of a
spirit of despair (Isa. 61:1-3).

SECTION 1:

THE PURSUIT OF BEAUTY

A thing of beauty is a joy forever;
its loveliness increases; it will never
pass into nothingness. . . .

JOHN KEATS (1795–1821)

Chapter 1

How Far Would You Go to Be Beautiful?

Life magazine reports that as many as 10 percent of college-age women, numbering a *million* or more, are thought to indulge in the self-destructive, secret practices of eating disorders. Many women of the nineties are preoccupied with beauty to the point of being shocking and sometimes lethal. Here are just a few real-life stories of the devastation that exists when the pursuit of beauty is out of control.

For years, I turned eating into an elaborate production — not to enhance my enjoyment of food, but to prevent myself from consuming too much.

As an anorexic, I devised schemes to delay the moment of intake, all on the theory that the slower I ate, the less food would ultimately enter my mouth. So, although I was right-handed, I fumbled through meals with a fork in my left hand instead. Sometimes I even awkwardly wielded chopsticks. I also diced all my food into almost-microscopic cubes, then swallowed only one at a time. I created other rituals, as well. If my meal consisted of several different foods, none could come into contact with the others, either on the plate or in my mouth.

By age 23, I was going to great extremes to avoid gaining weight. After working all day at my job in an accounts receivable department, I would desperately busy myself at home; straighten out closets, mop the bathroom — just to keep my mind off food. I let my hair grow long, expressly so that it would take me two hours to shampoo, condition, dry, and style it.

When you're anorexic, you're starved, and when you're starved, all you can think about — obsessively, torturously — is food. I thought about food all the time. What would I eat? When? How much?

After five years of near starvation, my health began to fail. My heart would palpitate. I felt dehydrated, exhausted, constantly agitated. It was difficult for me to keep a logical conversation going or to concentrate, either at my job or in school. I finally entered a hospital and, later, a long-term residential treatment center.

—Anonymous

Caroline Adams Miller writes about her bulimic practices:

I wanted to eat, I wanted to eat ice cream. I wanted it immediately. My brain, crammed moments before with facts for a history paper, clicked off. Nothing mattered now except getting my fix.

I pushed away notes and papers and looked outside. It was starting to snow. But tonight's bleak skies could do little to alter my plans. As I shut my books, I mentally rehearsed my now-familiar routine. On the way to Harvard Square, I would stop at the new ice cream shop. There I would get several scoops of some exotic flavor with Oreo cookies crushed in it. That would be Step One on this evening's self-destructive journey.

One of my earliest realizations that eating was not guilt-free came at age eight as I sat in a restaurant with my family in our town in Maryland. I heard my father say playfully to the waitress, "And the vanilla milk shake goes to the heavy one."

Although my father had been teasing, the remark firmly implanted itself in my brain, and I started looking in mirrors in a new way — turning this way and that, checking for a telltale bulge.

Eventually, I made a new enemy: the scale. More than once after stepping onto it — naked and before even a drop of water had crossed my lips in the morning, I dissolved into tears, cursing myself and my bloated body, resolving to be more vigilant in my pursuit of perfect thinness. But I was addicted to food.

Within two minutes, I was standing in line at the new ice cream store, scanning the choices I had already memorized. I knew I'd attract attention if I ordered four scoops. So I settled on a sedate coconut-chocolate combination with crushed Oreo cookies and took a seat in the corner.

Self-hatred began to fill me as I pushed my sundae glass away. Just that day I had been surveying my body in the mirror, vowing that I would drop at least one dress size by the time of my wedding in several months. I had written down instructions to myself about what to eat and what not to eat, ordering myself not to binge. Well, that resolve had disintegrated within a few hours. *You really are a loser if food has got such a grip on you*, I told myself as I stepped back outside to continue on my way.

Before my next food stop, I had to swing by the drugstore to get another tool I used in my endless quest to be thin — laxatives. I was planning to find a bathroom where I could throw up the thousands of calories I was in the process of ingesting. The massive doses of laxatives I would take afterward would scour out any remaining culprit calories. I wasn't planning to buy the laxatives, however. I was going to steal them, a habit I had fallen into early in my bulimic career because I hadn't wanted the drugstore clerks to suspect that I had an eating disorder. Stealing was a form of denial that I was abusing my body. If I wasn't actually buying the laxatives, I told myself, I wasn't really engaging in the crazy behavior.

The next stop on my compulsive journey that night was the gourmet cookie shop, where I gorged on chocolate cookies and stuffed my pockets full. Then I headed for another ice cream shop. As I walked in, I felt the tears starting in my eyes. I was out of control and nauseated from the richness of the food I had eaten, but I couldn't stop. I glanced at a couple next to me, each buying a single-dip vanilla cone. I was angry that they looked happy. I was also angry that they could order a single dip. I could no more order a single dip than an alcoholic could be contented with half a glass of wine.

When I'd finished, I threw my coat into the corner of the bathroom and looked in the mirror with disgust. My face looked pudgy. No cheekbones. I was breaking out, too. I had everything to live for, so why was I standing here in a bathroom again, angry, lonely, and depressed, with a grossly distended stomach and wishing I were dead?

I leaned over the antiseptic-smelling toilet bowl and held my hair back with my left hand. I jammed two fingers down my throat and felt the familiar bile rising. All of a sudden, the food came up in gushes, splattering all over the toilet seat, the floor and my clothes. Disgusted, yet elated at my success, I kept probing, trying to make sure I was getting everything up. To make the food come up faster, I balled my hand into a fist and punched my stomach hard, repeating it with a vengeance. I would have black-and-blue marks there tomorrow.

Finally, exhausted and filthy, I slumped on the floor and began to cry. *When will this all stop?* I wondered in despair as I laid my cheek against the cold floor and let the sobs overtake me. Worst of all was the knowledge that the degradation and pain would probably not prevent me from returning here tomorrow night to do the same thing again.

How is it that so many women are driven to the point of this kind of physical and emotional pain to gain thinness or what they would call beauty? What would motivate a person to such bizarre behaviors that could be devastating to health in so many ways?

Bulimia and or anorexia can upset the body's balance of electrolytes — such as sodium, magnesium, potassium, and calcium. This can cause fatigue, seizures, muscle cramps, irregular heartbeat, and decreased bone density, which can lead to osteoporosis. Repeated vomiting can damage the stomach and esophagus, causing the salivary glands to swell, the gums to recede, and the tooth enamel to erode. In some cases, all of the teeth must be pulled prematurely because of the constant wash by gastric acid.

Other effects may be rashes; broken blood vessels in the cheeks; swelling around the eyes, ankles, and feet; dry, thinning hair; baby-fine new hair growth along the hairline; dry lips, cracked at the corners; and bruises on the backs of the hand from purging.

It is interesting to note that the very tool used to gain physical beauty is also the tool that destroys beauty.

Denise De Garmo says that her eating disorder caused her gums to bleed. Blood filled her stools and urine and she developed erratic menstruation and an irregular heartbeat. Then one day in 1983, she woke up and discovered that her entire skin was wrinkled — the result of repeatedly vomiting muscle tissue. "I looked in the mirror," says Denise, "and I saw cottage cheese everywhere." Panicked, she checked into Rancho La Puerta, a fancy spa in Tecate, Mexico, hoping to firm her skin by taking off ten pounds."

As terrible as these symptoms and consequences may be, they seem to do little in motivating a woman driven to lose weight to actually quit. It's an obsession and an idol, and a sick-minded person will stop at nothing to accomplish thinness.

Such was the case for the famous recording artist of the seventies, Karen Carpenter; five foot four, 79 pounds. In some outfits, she was down to a size 0. She was bony high and low, her skin stretched over her hips, and her spine emerged like a string of buttons. She used syrup of ipecac to induce vomiting and died after a buildup of the drug irreversibly damaged her heart.

In *Cosmopolitan* (Jan. 1985), actress Jane Fonda revealed that she had been a secret bulimic from age 12 until her recovery at age 35 — sometimes binging and purging up to 20 times a day.

Fads and Eras of Image

In 1960, "Twiggy," the original waif, weighed 92 pounds, at 5'6". In 1970, Cheryl Tiegs, had a much bigger look and made a hit with her "great legs." The eighties epitomized fitness with supermodel Cindy Crawford. The nineties has gone back to the lean look with Kate Moss.

"Kate Moss and the new wave of wispy waif models are so skinny some critics believe they are selling anorexia and dangerous dieting," quotes the September 1993 issue of *People* magazine.

Kate Moss, a young, frail, British model weighs an estimated 100 pounds at 5'7". She left home at 17, and sometimes brings in as much as $10,000 a day. Apparently unconcerned with her weight, Moss claims to never weigh herself.

Moss and other ultra-thin models in the "waif wave" have stirred up quite a controversy, especially among parents of teenage girls. *People* magazine continues, "When *British Vogue* published an eight-page layout in June of the lank-haired, blank-eyed Moss — clad in scanty tank tops and tacky bikini panties as she posed in her very own unmade bed — the magazine drew bags of angry mail accusing it of encouraging everything from pedophilia to anorexia nervosa."

Andrea Tebay, 16, of Weston, Massachusetts, says, "My friends and I were looking at pictures of Kate. We thought we had to look like Cindy Crawford and now we have to look like this!"

Why are young (and older) women so bound by what society says is "the look"? Many of these "hot new models" have their pictures hanging up on countless walls where they are looked upon as *the image* and standard to attain. Glamour magazines are devoured and pored over as if they were the Bible itself. Could this be a form of modern idolatry?

Athletes and Eating Disorders

"Eating disorders are easily the gravest health problem facing female athletes, and they affect not just gymnasts but also swimmers, distance runners, tennis and volleyball players, divers and figure skaters," quotes *Sports Illustrated* in a special report on eating disorders. "According to the American College of Sports Medicine, as many as 62 percent of females competing in 'appearance' sports (such as figure skating and gymnastics) and endurance sports suffer from an eating disorder." Julie Anthony, a touring tennis pro in the seventies who now runs a sports-fitness clinic in Aspen, Colorado, has estimated that 30 percent of the women on the tennis tour suffer from some type of eating affliction. Peter Farrell, who has been coaching women's track and cross-country at Princeton for 17 years, puts the number of women runners with eating disorders even higher. "My experience is that *70 percent* of my runners have dabbled in its many hideous forms."

"For women, eating disorders are 'like steroids are

for men," says Liz Natale, a recovering anorexic who was a member of the Texas team that won the 1986 NCAA cross-country title. "You'll get results, but you'll pay for it."

Christy Henrich was "Dying for a Medal," according to *Sports Illustrated*'s special report. Christy Henrich, a promising young gymnast, died of multiple organ failure as a result of years of eating disorders. Her weight had plummeted as low as 47 pounds. Christy's parents were preparing to check her into the Menninger Clinic in Topeka, Kansas, two years before her death for treatment of her eating disorder. Moreno, Christy's fiancee, warned them to inspect her suitcase carefully. "It had a false bottom," he said. She had lined the entire bottom of the suitcase with laxatives. That was part of her addiction.

Henrich had been in and out of so many hospitals over the past two years that Moreno lost count of them. Her medical bills ran to more that $100,000.

Henrich told Dale Brendel of the *Independence Examiner* (Missouri), "My life is a horrifying nightmare. It feels like there's a beast inside me, like a monster. It feels evil."

Cathy Rigby, the 1972 Olympian who battled anorexia and bulimia for 12 years and twice went into cardiac arrest because of it, burst into tears at the news of Henrich's death. "I felt frustrated and angry," says Rigby, 40, who met Henrich as a TV commentator. "The sport is fertile ground for anorexia."

Gymnastics, at its highest level has evolved in a direction that is incompatible with a woman's mature body. Nadia Comaneci, the darling of the 1976 Olympics, proved that when she showed up at the world championships two years later having grown four inches and put on 21 pounds. She had become a woman. John Goodbody wrote in the *Illustrated History of Gymnastics*: "We learned that week how perfection in women's gymnastics can be blemished by maturity."

By the 1979 world championships, where she won the combined title, Comaneci was her old svelte self, having lost nearly 40 pounds in two months. Eating disorders originate in the mind, and like any disease of self-deception, they are difficult prisons to escape. That was suggested in 1990, in Barbara Grizzuti Harrison's story on Comaneci in *Life* magazine. "I'm fat and ugly," Comaneci, then 28, told the writer, although she was a size 6. When they went to dinner, Grizzuti Harrison wrote, "Her appetite for food is voracious. She eats her own food and [her companion] Constantin's, too. After each course, she goes to the bathroom. She is gone for a long time. She comes back, her eyes watery, picks her teeth, and eats some more. She eats mountains of raspberries and my creme brulee. She makes her way to the bathroom again. When she returns, she is wreathed in that rank sweet smell."

Keep clear of concealment,
keep clear of the need of concealment.
It is an awful hour when the first
necessity of hiding anything comes.
The whole life is different thenceforth.
When there are questions to be
feared and eyes to be avoided and
subjects which must not be touched,
then the bloom of life is gone.

PHILLIP BROOKS (1835–1893)

Chapter 2

What is an Eating Disorder?

An eating disorder is an abnormal relationship with food. A person who uses food to cope with life stresses has an eating disorder. The major eating disorders are anorexia, bulimia, binge-eating disorder (BED), and compulsive overeating. These eating disorders are classified as mental disorders. Obesity in itself is not a mental disorder, though some obese persons have eating disorders.

ANOREXIA (AN) is a disorder in which the individual deliberately acts to reach and maintain a below-normal body weight, is intensely afraid of gaining weight, and shows a disturbed and inaccurate perception of the size and shape of his or her body. Anorexic thought patterns and eating/exercise behavior obviously precede reaching anorexic weight, and it is important to seek treatment when these patterns and behaviors appear, and not wait for the extreme weight loss to seek a confirming diagnosis.

The anorexic believes herself to be fat or "just right" when everyone else sees her as shockingly thin. About 90 percent of anorexics are women, presumably because women in our culture are under greater pressure than men to be thin. Anorexia in men is the same as in women, with the obvious exception of loss of menses.

One marker of anorexia is amenorrhea — the absence of at least three consecutive menstrual cycles. Between 5 percent to 18 percent of anorexics die from the damaging effects of what is really prolonged starvation.

Types of anorexia include:

Anorexia — Restricting Type: During the current episode of anorexia, the person has not regularly engaged in binge-eating or in purging behavior (self-inducing vomiting or the misuse of laxatives, diuretics, or enemas).

Below-normal body weight is maintained almost entirely by restricting calorie intake.

Anorexia — Binge-eating/Purging type: During the current episode of anorexia, the person has engaged in binge-eating or purging. A large proportion of anorexics are also bulimic.

The Course of Anorexia

The course of anorexia nervosa is enormously variable. About 50 percent of hospitalized patients make a full psychological and physical recovery. But in a significant fraction of patients, anorexia nervosa is a fatal illness with death resulting from either inanition (physical condition caused by lack of food and water) or suicide. The death rate of patients once hospitalized for AN is probably between 5 percent and 20 percent, within 20 to 30 years after hospitalization. Between these two extremes lies a wide range of outcomes, with some patients leading a marginal existence in terms of both weight and psychological function and other patients only mildly impaired. Several studies suggest that an early age onset is more likely to be associated with a favorable outcome.

History: Anorexia has been known for at least 300 years, though the current cultural emphasis on dieting and thinness probably plays a part in the high frequency of eating disorders.

Clinical Characteristics: Anorexia usually begins in mid-adolescence, with a peak age of onset around 16 years. There is some tendency for children who eventually develop anorexia nervosa to be somewhat obsessive and shy beforehand. However, most patients show little or no serious psychopathology until the development of AN. The onset frequently seems precipitated (perhaps a last straw) by a minor trauma, such as leaving home for school or camp, the beginning of dating, or a casual unflattering remark.

Patients begin to diet in an apparent attempt to restore their self-esteem, and their dieting initially does not obviously differ from that of others who never develop psychological problems. However, in those who develop AN, the more weight that is lost, the more patients wish to lose. They typically become socially isolated and withdrawn, assume a moralistic demeanor, and become stubborn and intent on losing weight. Throughout the illness they exhibit an impressive denial of physical or psychological problems; this denial is often the most difficult aspect of starting treatment.

Patients retain some sensation of hunger until very late in the illness with the frequent occurrence of uncontrollable binge eating. At some point during the evolution of the illness, most patients with anorexia engage in increased physical activity, which serves both their intense drive for accomplishment and their desire to expend calories.

BULIMIA is a disorder in which the person has recurrent episodes of binge-eating and acts to prevent weight gain by self-induced vomiting or other compensatory behaviors.

1. Binge eating: An episode of binge eating includes

the following characteristics: a) eating, in a single time period, an amount of food that is definitely larger than most people would eat during a similar time period and under similar circumstances; and b) a sense of lack of control over eating during the episode.

Many people loosely self-define a "binge" as eating any food or quantity of food that does not conform to their personal diet rules — eating a muffin at coffee break, for example, when they had promised themselves never to eat at coffee break. This is not the clinical definition of a binge.

2. Recurrent inappropriate compensatory behavior in order to prevent weight gain, such as self-induced vomiting, misuse of laxatives, diuretics, enemas, or medications, fasting or excessive exercise. The binge eating and inappropriate compensatory behaviors both occur at least twice a week for three months.

Self-evaluation of one's worth as a person is unduly influenced by body shape and weight. The disordered self-evaluation does not occur exclusively during episodes of anorexia nervosa. Some bulimics are also anorexic.

Clinical Characteristics of Bulimia

Bulimia nervosa has been identified primarily in men and women in their teens and twenties, with about 90 percent women and 10 percent men (the same as for anorexia). Studies using rigorous diagnostic criteria suggest that about 1 percent to 2 percent of pre-college and college women are bulimic, although transient (occasional) sub-threshold (not meeting all criteria) bulimic behavior appears to be much more common (figures of 5 percent and more have been cited). Although the majority of patients who are currently diagnosed as bulimic are of normal weight, bulimia nervosa may be under-recognized in obese persons.

Binge Eating in Bulimia

The cardinal feature of a bulimic patient's eating pattern is a binge, which consists of a large amount of food eaten rapidly, usually with a sense of loss of control. Typical binge frequencies of patients who present themselves at eating disorders clinics range from 2 to 20 binges per week. Bulimic patients asked to binge in a monitored laboratory setting consumed more than 3,000 calories — over twice the amount consumed by non-bulimic controls asked to overeat.

Purging in Bulimia

Although the current diagnostic criteria for bulimia require only that patients regularly engage in some behavior designed to prevent weight gain, including fasting or vigorous exercise, most patients who receive the diagnosis engage in some form of active purging. Of purging methods, vomiting is the most common, almost 90 percent in one study, followed by laxative abuse (60 percent) and diuretic abuse (33 percent). Diet pill abuse is also commonly reported as a method of weight control.

Medical Complications of Bulimia

Outward signs of repeated self-induced vomiting include calluses on the back of the hand and fingers, salivary gland enlargement, and erosion of dental enamel. Fluid and electrolyte abnormalities, including dehydration occur frequently and can lead to disturbances of cardiac (heart) conduction and rhythm. Bulimic patients who use ipecac to induce vomiting can develop a potentially lethal cardiomyopathy (heart problems). Infrequent serious complications of repeated vomiting include esophageal or gastric rupture and pneumomediastinum. Longstanding laxative abuse can lead to laxative dependence and severe constipation.

Neuroendocrine Abnormalities

Menstrual disturbances often afflict even normal-weight bulimic patients, and in other ways, despite being at a statistically normal weight, these patients may show physiological similarities to underweight anorectic patients.

Clinical Course of Bulimia

Because bulimia nervosa has been recognized as a clinical entity for only about ten years, more is known about its onset than about its long-term outcome. The vast majority of patients (85 percent) begin binge eating during a period of dieting. Although the natural course of untreated bulimia is yet unknown, treatment studies have begun to report follow-up data on patients who have completed various treatment programs.

The most encouraging reports derive from psychotherapeutic treatment (individual or group therapy) studies that report continued improvement in most patients at one year after treatment. Follow-up data from medication studies, when provided, are somewhat less favorable, with many patients relapsing after discontinuation of medication.

Types of bulimia include:

Bulimia — Purging type: During the current episode of bulimia, the person has regularly engaged in self-induced vomiting or the misuse of laxatives, diuretics, or enemas.

Bulimia — Non-purging type: During the current episode of bulimia, the person has used other inappropriate compensatory behaviors, such as fasting or excessive exercise, but has not regularly engaged in self-induced vomiting or the misuse of laxatives, diuretics, or enemas.

BINGE-EATING DISORDER (BED) is recurrent episodes of binge eating. An episode of binge eating is characterized by both of the following:

1. Eating, in a single time period an amount of food that is definitely larger than most people would eat during a similar time period and under similar circumstances.

2. A sense of lack of control over eating during the episode. The binge-eating episodes are associated with three or more of the following:

        A. Eating much more rapidly than normal.

        B. Eating until feeling uncomfortably full.

        C. Eating large amounts of food when not feeling physically hungry.

        D. Eating alone because of being embarrassed by how much one is eating.

        E. Feeling disgusted with oneself, depressed or very guilty after overeating.

Marked distress regarding binge eating is present. The binge eating occurs, on average, at least two days a week for six months. The binge eating is not associated with the regular use of inappropriate compensatory behaviors (such as purging, fasting, excessive exercise) and does not occur exclusively during the course of anorexia nervosa or bulimia nervosa.

COMPULSIVE OVEREATING : The person experiences an inability to stop eating and a craving to eat more regardless of fullness.

In this chapter you may have recognized some of the same or similar behaviors in yourself from one of the following descriptions: anorexia, bulimia, binge-eating disorder, or compulsive overeating.

It is important for your well-being in every way to be honest with yourself. To help you know if you have and eating disorder, read the following information, figure out your own Body Mass Index with a calculator and complete the questions.

Anorexia: According to Online's Frequently Asked Questions for Eating Disorders, "Anorexic weight is 15 percent or more below normal. A body mass chart indicates a healthy 5' 9" man may weigh as little as 140 pounds, below that he is under weight, and 120 pounds is crossing the borderline from underweight to anorexic. For a 5' 5" woman, about 122 is the borderline between healthy and underweight; below about 108, she is judged anorexic."

Body Mass Index

Are you anorexic? Obese? Underweight? Is your weight in the healthy range for your height? The BMI (Body Mass Index) is one way to tell. The formula is: Body Mass Index equals body weight in kilograms divided by the square of height in meters. Check your weight and height without clothes or shoes:

    1. Divide your weight in pounds by 2.2, to get your weight in kilograms. (Ex: 130 lbs./2.2 = 59 kilograms.)

    2. Divide your height in inches by 39.4 to get your height in meters. (Ex: 65 inches/39.4

= 1.65 meters.) Now square this number. (Ex: 1.65 x 1.65 = 2.72.)

3. Divide weight number by the height number (height squared). That's your BMI. (Ex: 59 kilograms / 2.72 =21.7 BMI.)

My BMI is: _____

Okay, so you've got your number, now what does it mean? A booklet distributed by some eating disorder programs gives these ranges:

What Your Body Mass Index Means

	Women	Men
Anorexic:	Below 16	Below 16
Underweight:	16-19	16-19
Healthy:	19-25	19-26.5
Mild Obesity:	25-35	26.5-35
Severe Obesity:	over 35	over 35

There is a lot of latitude within the categories to allow for variations in frame size and body type. Give yourself some slack for your own unique body and metabolism, but be realistic concerning if your BMI is out of the healthy range in either direction.

This series of questions may help you determine if you are a compulsive overeater (or possibly bulimic). Many members of Overeaters Anonymous have found that they have answered yes to many of these questions:

1. Do you eat when you're not hungry?

2. Do you go on eating binges for no apparent reason?

3. Do you have feelings of guilt and remorse after overeating?

39

THE PURSUIT OF BEAUTY

4. Do you give too much time and thought to food?

5. Do you look forward with pleasure and anticipation to the time when you can eat alone?

6. Do you plan these secret binges ahead of time?

7. Do you eat sensibly before others and make up for it alone?

8. Is your weight affecting the way you live your life?

9. Have you tried to diet for a week (or longer), only to fall short of your goal?

10. Do you resent others telling you to "use a little willpower" to stop overeating?

11. Despite evidence to the contrary, have you continued to assert that you can diet "on you own" whenever you wish?

12. Do you crave to eat at a definite time, day or night, other than mealtime?

13. Do you eat to escape from worries or trouble?

14. Have you ever been treated for obesity or a food-related condition?

15. Does your eating behavior make you or others unhappy?

©1986, 1989 Overeaters Anonymous, Inc.

Are you anorexic?_____
Bulimic?_____
Have Binge-eating Disorder?_____
An Overeater?_____
Low Self-esteem?_____

Beware of no man more
than yourself; we carry
our worst enemies with us.

CHARLES HADDON SPURGEON (1834–1892)

Chapter 3

Where My Story Begins

"All you have to do is eat cheese and fruits and the pounds will just drop off!" My ears perked up. I was sitting in the high school cafeteria, eating a chocolate milkshake and fries. I had just overheard a conversation between two of the older popular girls at school who I admired. As a 16-year-old sophomore, I desperately wanted to look like those tall, slim models I compared myself to in different glamour magazines. The tall part I couldn't change, being 4' 11", but the slim part . . . ! At that point, I made a decision that opened the door to the greatest battle of my life.

I was growing up in Colorado and had been a pretty secure kid. School, friends, skiing, and boys were my life. My family provided a great amount of my confidence and security. My parents and grandparents were very supportive, loving, and affectionate people. We spent hours together, playing games, eating, laughing, and talking. I have some of the best memories spending Christmas up in my grandparents quaint little condominium in the mountains. The snowflakes were as big as quarters and would fall so quietly and melt on our noses as we walked to the little country church for the midnight service to sing Christmas carols. Life was easy and simple.

But when I was 13, a devastating thing happened to our family that shook us all to the core. My parents divorced. It affected everyone in our family severely. Trust was broken, hurt set in, and my perfect little world was shattered. None of us would ever be the same again.

Soon after my parents separated, I began to party, withdraw from my family, and guard my heart from any more hurts. It was the saddest time in my life. I was lonely, empty, and bored. I was close to no one. I didn't know how to be honest about my feelings and I could not open up to the very closest people in my life.

I began hanging out with a different crowd who I felt more comfortable with. They "didn't care" about their families either. We would go to concerts, get high, and have fun. I remember thinking, *Smoking pot has nothing to do with trying to avoid my problems. Besides, the divorce doesn't affect me a bit.* (Interesting coincidence.)

I remember feeling especially insecure around my dad. All of a sudden I felt lost and cut off from a once very close relationship. He was remarried to a beautiful, smart, and skinny woman; everything I wanted to be for my dad.

At the same time all of these events were taking place in my life, unbeknownst to me, a very loving Heavenly Father had a plan which included me, and He was about to intervene. God can turn some of the most devastating times in our lives into jewels when He comes on the scene.

Some close friends of our family began sharing some things with us that changed us forever and our hearts were primed for answers.

I'd always known the "story" about Jesus Christ's death and resurrection and believed it to be true, but it didn't affect my lifestyle in the least. I'd gone to church all of my life: of course I believed in God — who didn't? But what I didn't know was that He wasn't as boring as I thought church was. He wasn't that dusty old ancient-looking Moses guy that was about ready to pass out any moment from his own uninvolvement with his people. It was a revelation to me that Jesus Christ was vibrant and *alive*, and cared about exactly what I was going through. It intrigued me that He knew the number of hairs on my head and that He wanted to be very involved in every area in my life; to become my personal friend, Father, and Saviour. I didn't know about repenting of my sins and being reconciled back to God. Theology didn't make much sense to me; all I knew was that I needed a Father, now. I came running to the altar and finally poured out my heart to my Heavenly Daddy.

[God is] A Father to the fatherless (Ps. 68:5).

Recovery Workbook: Lesson 2
Live It Out!

Take a moment to examine your own heart before God. Even if you are painfully bound to an eating disorder, your relationship with God is of higher priority. Without Him, you will never be truly free, anyway.

Have you ever received His forgiveness and acknowledged that He is your maker, your Saviour from sin and death, and the Lord of your life?

If you were the only person living on this earth, He would have died and suffered for you, because He loves you that deeply. He took the penalty (which we each deserve because of our sin) of death and died in our place.

The good news is, if we believe this with all of our heart and choose to follow Him, we can have true life: His presence and peace in our lives here on earth, and eternal life with Him forever. We don't have to live in spiritual death like Adam and Eve experienced in the Garden of Eden when they disobeyed God. We can walk with Him and talk with Him all of our lives and throughout eternity.

First Step to Recovery
Get Right with God

If you've never received Jesus in your heart, do it now. That is the first step to your recovery and the greatest decision of your life. Talk to Him as a friend. Pour out your heart honestly before Him, hiding nothing, because He knows every thought before you speak it. If you pray with true sincerity of heart, the Bible says you become a child of God and a new creation. You are forgiven and are washed clean. God gives you a brand new start. This is only the beginning of a beautiful love relationship between you and your Heavenly Father.

"Come now, let us reason together," says the Lord. "Though your sins are like scarlet, they shall be as white as snow; though they are red as crimson, they shall be like wool. If you are willing and obedient, you will eat the best from the land; but if you resist and rebel, you will be devoured by the sword" (Isa. 1:18-19).

"Believe in the Lord Jesus Christ, and you will be saved — you and your household" (Acts 16:31).

If you don't know how to pray to receive Jesus as your Lord and Saviour, you can pray this prayer:

Lord Jesus, I believe that You died just for me. I know that I am not right with God, and so I ask that You would forgive me of all my sin and make me clean inside. I believe that You rose from the dead and are alive forever! Right now, I commit my whole heart and life to You, to live *only* for You from this day forth. Thank You for loving me and accepting me, just how I am, and for making me Your child. In the name of Jesus, AMEN!

Fill in the date you prayed to receive Jesus:

_____

But God demonstrates his own love for us in this: While we were still sinners, Christ died for us. Since we have now been justified by his blood, how much more shall we be saved from God's wrath through him! (Rom. 5:8).

If you prayed that prayer sincerely with your heart, then you are a new person! "Therefore, if anyone is in Christ, he is a new creation; the old has gone, the new has come!" (2 Cor. 5:17).

The Spirit of the living Lord has come to make His home within your heart, and He promises never to leave you or forsake you. He has given you His own righteousness which simply means you are now right with God. This righteousness from God comes through faith in Jesus Christ to all who believe . . . for all have sinned and fall short of the glory of God, and are justified freely by His grace through the redemption that came by Christ Jesus.

No good works that we do have the power to make us right with God. Only accepting the free gift of His Son and believing in Him enough to follow Him will insure eternal life. From this day forth, your life will never be the same.

If you have received Jesus before, but are not walking closely with Him now, don't wait another minute, running from the One who knows and loves you most. Make a fresh commitment right now to love and follow Him no matter what the cost. You won't regret your decision.

Growing in the Lord

Our friends told us how God would give us a new start, heal our brokenness, and show us His awesome plan for our lives. We discovered that we weren't really fighting against each other; it was Satan, the enemy of our souls, who was trying to destroy us.

> The thief comes only to steal, kill and destroy; I have come that they may have life and have it to the full" (John 10:10).

So many people spend years with a psychologist, blaming God or other people for the bad things that happen in their lives because they don't understand that "the devil prowls around like a roaring lion, looking for someone to devour" (1 Pet. 5:8).

As soon as I submitted my life to the Lord, I began to understand the authority I had over Satan. Luke 10:19 says, "I have given you authority to trample on snakes and scorpions and to overcome all the power of the enemy; nothing will harm you." I became an overcomer rather than constantly being defeated by life's ups and downs.

I learned to pray about everything, the little and the

big. One time my favorite dog, Higgins, a miniature schnauzer, was deathly ill. Several vets had already told us that there was nothing that could be done for Higgins. She had always been very playful and active, but now she was dull and listless. She couldn't even get up and down the stairs.

My mother came to me and Glen, my brother, and told us about a book she had read. In the book, another family had prayed for a sick gerbil and God actually healed that rat-like creature. She said that if God cared for a gerbil, He certainly cared for our Higgins. Glen and I thought she had lost her mind when she had us circle around Higgins and lay our hands on her to pray. But we did it to pacify our dear, crazy mom. Well, our eyes just about popped out of our head when after our prayer, Higgins jumped up and ran around in circles, jumped on the bed, ran up and down the stairs, and was completely healed. I never again wondered if something was too small or insignificant for our loving Lord.

Our family saw miracles almost daily, and I knew God was real and that He had a plan for my life.

One evening I came into my mother's room and confessed to her that the friends I presently had were not good influences on me, but that I didn't have the strength to influence them for the Lord. My wise mother said, "Well then, let's pray for new friends!"

Soon after that, I joined a Bible study group and slowly stepped out of my old friends' lives. It was too difficult for me to live an on-fire Christian life around them anymore. I met seven new Christian friends in the Bible study who helped me stay accountable and strong throughout my entire high school years.

Another major change came as I gave up my precious music. Pink Floyd, Led Zepplin, and Aerosmith were some of my favorites, yet it began to occur to me that their words swimming around in my head were not glorifying to God, nor did they help me get any closer to where I wanted to go in life.

It was a tough decision, especially because there were not a lot of Christian groups who played the style of music I liked as a teenager, but I wanted more than anything to keep my thoughts pure and on the Lord. I came to the point where I chose to put nothing in my mind except those things that would help me grow stronger. Looking back, the implications of that decision were profound. The words which play in our minds actually make up who we become.

I developed a strong quiet time, a daily period of time I set aside to seek God, sing to Him, to listen to His voice, and read His Word. He became my best friend. My life was radically changing by a living God.

Recovery Workbook: Lesson 3
Live It Out!

The last section you read referred to a *quiet time*; a daily amount of time that you set aside to spend time with the Lord. Your relationship with Jesus will grow, only as you spend time with Him. This is not a religion you've bound yourself to, but a person, and like any other healthy relationship with a person, this, the highest priority of all your relationships, needs nurturing. In order to get to know God, you need to communicate with Him. This communication is called prayer.

David, of the Bible, was said to be a man after God's own heart. He spent hours when he was a boy and throughout his adult life with the Lord, singing songs about and to Him, meditating on His goodness, and pouring his heart out to God. The majority of the Psalms in the Old Testament were written by David during his times set aside to be with God.

Jesus himself was another example of someone who spent the majority of the time in His 24-hour days with God, His Father. He only did what He had seen His Father doing in prayer. In John 5:19-20 He said, "I tell you the truth, the Son can do nothing by himself; he can do only what he sees his Father doing, because whatever the Father does the Son also does."

If you desire deep intimacy with the Lord, begin by setting aside a certain amount of time daily to spend with Him. Make it different everyday so that it never becomes monotonous. You may want to take a walk, write prayers in your journal, listen to a Christian worship tape and worship God along with the tape, or do a Bible study. It's important to include prayer, worship, *and Bible reading* in your daily quiet time to make sure you stay on track and don't get caught up in false doctrines. The Bible is our standard of belief, not experience.

Be honest with God and feel free to pour out your heart to Him. Then quiet your heart and listen for His still, small voice. He promises to speak to His own children. "His sheep follow him because they know his voice" (John 10:4). He will never contradict what He has already said in His Word, the Bible.

Here are some Scriptures on quiet times from the Psalms to help you get started:

> Out of the depths I cry to you, O Lord; O Lord, hear my voice. Let your ears be attentive to my cry for mercy (Ps. 130:1-2).

I do not concern myself with great matters

or things too wonderful for me. But I have stilled and quieted my soul like a weaned child with its mother, like a weaned child is my soul within me (Ps. 131:1-2).

I lift up my eyes to the hill, where does my help come from? My help comes from the Lord, the Maker of heaven and earth (Ps. 121:1-2).

He who dwells in the shelter of the Most High will rest in the shadow of the Almighty (Ps. 91:1).

1. Make a commitment to begin having a quiet time daily: Write out the amount of time you will begin with and what time of the day:

_____

2. Get a PRAYER JOURNAL. There are many uses for a prayer journal such as:

    a. The obvious — writing out your prayers when you find it difficult to pray.
    b. Any time you feel you have heard from the Lord, write it down!
    c. Special Scriptures that you are memorizing or meditating on.
    d. Taking down good sermon notes!
    e. Any significant spiritual experience.

3. Get rid of things in your life that pull you away from the Lord.

This is completely between you and God. Let the Holy Spirit deal with you in His timing, but respond when

He deals with you. Christianity is not a set of rules to be followed. Again, it is a relationship with Jesus. But there are things in all of our lives that we need to get rid of. Some things are definitely wrong such as drinking alcohol under age or in excess, drugs, promiscuous clothing, ungodly relationships or friendships, and blatantly blasphemous music, standing against every godly virtue.

Other things may be okay for some, but they're not okay for you if your life is out of balance or what you are doing may be hindering your spiritual life, (such as TV). If God is dealing with you on an issue, don't ignore Him, He knows what's best for you and will always replace whatever it is that you are giving up with something better.

> Therefore, since we are surrounded by such a great cloud of witnesses, let us throw off everything that hinders and the sin that so easily entangles, and let us run with perseverance the race marked out for us. Let us fix our eyes on Jesus (Heb. 12:1-2).

Make a list of the things you want to give up in order to live a holy life for the Lord:

_____

_____

_____

_____

> Then Jesus said to his disciples, "If anyone would come after me, he must deny himself and take up his cross and follow me" (Matt. 16:24).

Bulimia

Although I allowed God to change my life in obvious areas of sin, there were other, more hidden areas in my heart that Satan was working on to destroy me. He was not going to give up so easily. If he cannot pull a person away from the Lord in one area, he will try another. That's exactly what happened to me. I had a blind spot that I had not yet dealt with. In fact, I didn't know I needed to. The Bible says, "*My people* are destroyed from lack of knowledge" (Hos. 4:6). In other words, even *Christians* can be destroyed in certain areas of their lives if they don't have the knowledge of God's Word, the only real truth, being lived out.

My self-esteem had been shattered. As much as I loved and respected my parents, my trust and security was broken apart. In fact, their self-esteem had been shattered as well. Divorce affects every member of the family and no matter how strong the individual may be, at some point in their life they will have to deal with rejection, hurt, and unforgiveness. No one can just sail through and expect to weather a divorce with no scars.

Although separation and other dysfunctions seem to be the plight of most American families, it was never God's intention. God meant for family relationships, although imperfect, to be a haven, a refuge, and a support system for each human being. We all need that security and love, and when we don't live by God's Word, our needs do not get met, and we look to other things to fill our hearts. Because we live in a fallen world where Satan rules the kingdoms of this earth (see Matt. 4:8), people succumb to temptation and life has its challenges. Only through God can there be real healing.

As the years went by, my self-esteem grew worse, without my even realizing it. Although I seemed confident on the outside, I began to doubt my opinions and compare myself to everyone else. I didn't understand who I was or the purpose of my life. I hadn't received the healing that God would have so readily given. I was dying for lack of knowledge and Satan had his foot in the door.

At first I was restless and wanted to be different than I was — more attractive, thinner, smarter, more athletic, you name it; I was not satisfied with anything about myself. Really, I wasn't overweight, but because my heart was so unsatisfied, I thought if I could just lose at least ten pounds I'd be totally happy!

I began to diet. I so wanted the approval of my father which I didn't think I had. I was determined to lose weight, because in my mind I would gain his and everyone else's acceptance if I did.

I joined several exercise classes at different times and figured out that an 800 calorie a day diet would get the results I wanted. My weight, like most everybody else on a strict diet, fluctuated constantly.

I tried eating only cheese and fruit for a while like my popular anorexic friends suggested, but self-control in the eating department was not my forte and I hated getting headaches and feeling so hungry and weak all of the time. Besides that, I wanted quicker results.

Finally I became so desperate that I didn't care what it took. I would be thin. When diet pills, starving myself, and regular dieting were not working for me, I tried something else. Some other girls I knew at school were eating whatever they wanted and then throwing it up without gaining any weight. Eating everything you want without the consequences! What a perfect solution for someone who loved to eat as much as me! But what a lie from the pit of hell. Little did I know then that the consequences would be a thousand times worse than the pleasures of eating or being thin.

It started out gradually at the end of my high school years. I would come home from a hard day of school, grab a carton of ice cream and plop down in front of the TV, not paying any attention to the amount I was eating. All of a sudden, panic would hit me when I thought about what I had just done, and I would run to the bathroom to get rid of all those calories.

After several similar episodes, I began to plan out my binges. I really never lost any weight doing this, in fact, I gained weight. My throat hurt and I felt so guilty that I told my Mom.

She was so concerned about me that she made me go to several different counselors. It was always the same story: I'd sit down in front of a total stranger, tell my whole life story, and then wait for their professional opinion. No one ever seemed to know what to do with me and I grew weary of sharing my guts, but getting no answers. Maybe I really didn't want help.

So . . . I went on to college. My mother hoped things would be better for me at a Christian college.

No one knew me, and I liked it that way. The closer people got, the more they would see my ugly habit, so I kept people on a surface level. The rest of my life was going downhill, but my eating disorder developed into an art.

A doctor told me that I had actually trained my stomach to go the other way. Although I had become very proficient in eating whatever I wanted and still maintaining my desired weight, I was living a kind of hell on earth. I'd go to classes and then every spare moment I'd sneak away for about two hours to a secret world where I didn't have to think or care.

I had no meaningful relationships, but I was still desperately caught up in the way I looked. At one point, I was running 8 miles a day on a cross-country team and had gotten down to 85 pounds. I was binging and purging as many as five times a day. My mind would be in sort of a trance. This dream world was the way I handled stress and fears, but in reality I wasn't handling anything. I was exactly like an alcoholic, except when things went wrong for me, I'd go to the grocery store instead of the bottle.

Bulimia only magnified my problems and caused me to slip into a deep depression. I no longer lived in reality, but pulled away from everything and everyone dear to me who could help me. The lack of love and rejection I felt were my own perceptions, because I had not received the healing I needed from God. Many times I'd feel like a living dead person, just going through the motions of life.

SECTION 2:

TRANSFORMED!

Breathe on me, breath of God;
Fill me with life anew,
That I may love what thou dost love,
And do what thou wouldst do.

EDWIN HATCH (1835-1889)

Chapter 4

How I Overcame Bulimia

It had been five long years. I was beginning to doubt that God even cared anymore, let alone anyone else. I had tried everything I knew to do. I went to an eating disorder support group, a psychologist, counselors, and was prayed for to receive "deliverance." My friends held me accountable for what I ate. A thousand resolutions later, nothing seemed to work. I knew why I felt rejected, why I wanted to be thin, but I didn't know how to get over my eating problem.

Every relationship I had, suffered. The most painful was my relationship with the Lord. I knew I was breaking His heart. I must have asked His forgiveness ten thousand times, but I could not quit.

I gave up hope. I told the Lord that I couldn't make any more plans or goals to change — He would have to change me himself.

One day I was crying to a friend of mine, (who later became my life-long friend and husband), "God must hate me! Why won't He *help me*?" Ron told me something that I've never forgotten, and I've told countless others the same thing since. He said, "You don't know how God

63

sees you. You need to find out from His Word!"

That statement began to really bug me. Of course I knew that God loved me, He loved everybody. And besides that, I read the Bible everyday. So why did Ron say that?

Obviously, he meant something deeper than my understanding at that time.

I began to look up specific Scriptures that dealt with the way that my Heavenly Father viewed me. I wrote every one of them down and read them over and over again. I'd say them out loud to myself. I thought about them. I memorized them. I carried note cards to class and read them to myself when I got bored. I *devoured* them like a starving person would his first taste of food. I had been starving; actually dying spiritually, and these words were life to me. It was as if scales began to fall off my eyes. The Scripture came alive to me. It became my food, my air, my sustenance, my very life. I clung to the truths I was finding. It transformed my thinking about everything, especially about myself. After years of being bound to self-hatred, God's truth began to set me free.

Words for Reflection

The cords of death entangled me, the torrents of destruction overwhelmed me. . . . In my distress I called to the Lord. I cried to my God for help. . . . He reached down from on high and took hold of me; he drew me out of deep waters. He rescued me from my powerful enemy. . . . He rescued me because *He delighted in me* (Ps. 18:4, 6, 19).

Praise the Lord, O my soul, and forget not all his benefits — who forgives all your sins and heals all your diseases. Who redeems your life from the pit and crowns you with love and compassion (Ps. 103:2-4).

You turned my wailing into dancing, you removed my sackcloth and clothed me with joy, that my heart may sing to you and not be silent (Ps. 3:11-12).

We achieve inner health only
through forgiveness — the
forgiveness not only of others
but also of ourselves.

JOSHUA LOTH LIEBMAN (1907–1948)

Chapter 5

Wholeness through Forgiveness

Second Step to Recovery

The following story is from a dear friend of mine, Michelle, who is struggling to overcome her past and her eating disorder:

> My childhood was not a happy one. I don't remember smiling, laughing, or the simple freedom of being a child. I don't remember innocence because it was stolen from me at such a young age. I don't remember love or parental touch. I don't remember affirmations. I do remember chaos, screaming, yelling . . . abuse.
>
> When I was 11 years old, I was sexually abused by a man I completely trusted. I had no weird feelings about him, no indication that anything was wrong. He treated me like I was truly loved and cherished. It felt great to me. But then to have him sexually abuse me cut me

69

very deeply. I was not expecting it at all. I had none of my protectors up. It's like someone is violently raping you, but at the same time, their face shows care and concern as if to ask if you're okay. My mind couldn't handle that. I could not understand. So I made a conscious decision, outright, that I would never think or talk about it again. I became a stone. I took control. That control took the form of an eating disorder. Consequently, I began starving myself because it satisfied this . . . need. This hurt and pain deep within me. I felt it gave me strength in some odd way.

Such is the sad plight of so many young ladies and gentlemen who struggle with low self-esteem and eating disorders.

We are the culmination of our childhood experiences: our happenstances, what we've been taught, the words that have been spoken to us, and the examples of our family members. So much of who we are has to do with who our parents or guardians are, their character, how they view life, their habits, and their lifestyle. Whether we agree with them or not, they have had strong influences on us, especially through the impressionable ages of one through five. The Bible says, "Train a child in the way he should go and when he is old, he will not depart from it" (Prov. 22:6). God meant for parents to be the main influences of children. If your parents did not know the Lord and train you in His ways, they were automatically training you in *their* ways. Training takes place, whether pro-active or unintentional, and good or bad, those impressions stick.

However, as we get older we decide the direction our lives will take and it is we, not our parents, who are accountable to God for who we will become. My dad always says, "You are who you are because of your parents; if you choose to stay that way, it's because of you."

You may have had very difficult experiences growing up, maybe even as tragic as the stories I've written about, but that does not mean you are bound to broken emotions for the rest of your life. My husband Ron had a devastating childhood, but he did not let that dictate who he would become. He was determined to forgive and go on with his life, living for Jesus, with a bright future ahead.

Unfortunately, many people live a life of bitterness and unforgiveness. They become exactly what they despise in their parents or other people who have hurt them, because they have not forgiven. We have seen abuse victims abuse their own children, and children of alcoholics become alcoholics themselves or marry an alcoholic. It's a sad scenario. You'd think they would run far the other direction, but this is the fruit of unforgiveness.

While some are fortunate enough to have had loving, supportive families and strong Christian influence even from a young age these days, most are not. Through years of counseling teenagers, we've seen that the majority of their problems stem from family relationships. The family is where they've received their understanding of who they are and who God is. I believe that the root causes of eating disorders, such as unforgiveness and self-hatred, stem directly from poor family relationships. It's a fact that bulimics and anorexics most times come from families of abuse, alcoholism, or divorce.

I've also seen the other extreme, where people set out in search of themselves, dwelling on their past and spending hours in clinics, desperately trying to feel better about themselves and understand why they are the way they are. I say this very carefully because I know there are good Christian counselors available to help with emotional healing and some people need an objective party to

71

help them sort through their feelings and experiences.

But I truly believe that many, many people are wasting their money and their counselor's time because they refuse to accept biblical answers. Where in the Bible does it say to spend half your life "finding yourself" or spending time getting healing from different expert psychologists and psychiatrists? Who is the Great Healer?

Do you know what the Bible says to do if you've been mistreated, abused, neglected, or hurt? It says to *forgive*. Forgive your enemies. Don't hold on to bitterness or anger or rage. Yes, you've been mistreated. It wasn't fair. It wasn't your fault. You may have been five years old, how could it have possibly been your fault? But if you choose to hold on to the past, to hold on to those hurts, it won't hurt anyone but yourself. Unforgiveness is like a cancer. If it is not dealt with, it will begin to infect every area of your life. It is deadly and it will cost you everything, even eternal life.

People are imperfect. Everyone makes mistakes — some more than others, but if you put your ultimate faith and trust in people, they will fail you. God wants you to trust Him. He promises that He'll never fail you or forsake you. But it is now up to you to quit shifting the blame for all your problems onto your parents or anyone else who may have hurt you. It's time to begin taking responsibility for who you are going to become.

In doing that, you may have to get very honest with yourself and with God and spend some significant time praying over events and people who have hurt you.

I had to come to that place in my own life where I chose to forgive and quit blaming other people. I came to grips with the fact that I would never get over bulimia until I chose to make it happen. I would no longer be a victim. My life would be what I made it. That was the beginning of healing for me.

Recovery Workbook: Lesson 4
Live It Out!

Forgiveness is such a miraculous gift from God. All it requires from us is an act of our will. God forgave us while we were all undeserving, now He requires us to do the same. Scripture says that if we do not forgive, we will not be forgiven (Matt 6:14-15). That's a pretty serious statement — the difference between heaven and hell.

Once we have chosen to forgive, God will meet us halfway with His grace. We can then actually begin to see those who have hurt us the way God sees them and be free of all our pain. I have seen, time and again, how victims of every kind of abuse imaginable, who have forgiven the offender, can actually think of the horrible memories without shedding a tear. They have truly forgiven and freedom has come. It can and will happen to you if you will surrender completely to God and choose to forgive every offense.

Mrs. Nancy Cole, wife of Dr. Edwin Cole, has a very effective way to tangibly forgive. Take out your prayer journal and on one of the pages make three columns. In the left column, write down every person who has ever hurt you, who you have not yet forgiven. In the middle column, write exactly what they did or said to hurt you. Maybe someone said something that triggered your whole eating disorder. Write it down. In the right hand column, write down how it made you feel. This is so that you can identify exactly what you are forgiving and there are no wounds left untouched that can fester into bitterness. Now, very prayerfully, think through each person and event. The Lord is right beside you and will help you recall old memories that you may have suppressed. This may take a good amount of time and may be quite painful at first, but the Lord is faithful to walk through it with you if you really desire to be healed and whole. Now, begin to release your rights to be angry and to hold a bitter grudge. Let the Lord Jesus give you the grace to forgive and love your enemies. When you're completely finished, confess your victory: "The blood of Jesus has cleansed me and this is never to be remembered against me or this person again." You may even want to take a red marker and mark out each event, covering it with the "blood of Jesus." When and if those feelings of hurt or bitterness ever rise up again, you can declare with confidence, "NO! I forgave that person on _____ (whatever date) and I will not hold anything against them ever again." It is an act of your will, not based on emotion or feelings. *YOU ARE FREE!*

A handful of the earth
to make God's image!

ELIZABETH BARRETT BROWNING (1806–1861)

Chapter 6

Transformed!

Third Step to Recovery

Deliverance is an incredible thing. I look back on my life now and can hardly believe I was the person I was 12 years ago. That is how awesome our God is. When He heals, He leaves no scars. "When the Son sets you free, you are free indeed" (John 8:36). Believe me when I say, *you* can be healed. *You* can change. It doesn't matter how "far gone" you are or feel. Jesus Christ is greater! He can pull you out of the deepest pit and make you a brand new person.

For some, all it takes is a prayer to be set free. For me, it was different. I believe in prayer, good biblical counsel, accountability, and spiritual warfare. It takes all of these things and more to walk a solid Christian life. But in my case, instant answers didn't come. Bulimia was not only the result of sin in my life, but it had become a stronghold that Satan used to destroy the plan God had for me. I couldn't just decide to repent. I had to launch an all-out attack on the enemy to destroy the stronghold. Second Corinthians 10:4 explains it perfectly:

> The weapons we fight with are not the weapons of this world. On the contrary, they have divine power to demolish strongholds. We demolish arguments and every pretension that sets itself up against the knowledge of God and we take captive every *thought* to make it obedient to Christ.

Satan doesn't come to us in a little red suit and horns to seduce us. His battleground is within our minds. He tries to influence our thinking, specifically making accusations and arguments against the *knowledge of God*, or the Word of God. When we believe him over the Word of God, Satan is able to cause us to sin. The progression of sin is this:

> THOUGHT
> DESIRE
> ATTITUDE
> ACTION
> HABIT
> STRONGHOLD

> But each one is tempted when, by his own evil desire, he is dragged away and enticed. Then, after desire is conceived, it gives birth to sin; and sin, when it is full grown, gives birth to death (James 1:14-15).

If sin is continued long enough, it can eventually lead to death.

Instead of turning to God for healing in the midst of my desperation, I considered thoughts Satan planted in my mind. "If I could just be thinner, I'd feel so much better about myself. I'm no good. I'm ugly. Why do I always have to say such stupid things?" Then when the idea of bulimia was presented to me, it seemed like a way out. I actually believed lies over all the precious promises of God. The problem was *I didn't know* those promises. I was "dying for lack of knowledge" (Hos. 4:6).

Destroying the Strongholds

The world always tries to "fix" a problem from the outside. In other words, if you're bulimic, just eat less. If you're anorexic, eat more. You feel lousy about yourself? Well then, just go on this new diet, or that aerobics plan! Change your hairstyle, your wardrobe! Get a boyfriend. Take drugs! Party! You'll be happy when you get married!

It won't work!

We were meant to be motivated, energized, and transformed from the inside out. To tell me to stop eating and throwing up was just like taking a drunk off the street, cleaning him up, putting him in a suit, taking his bottle away, and saying, "Okay, now go live a healthy, productive life." Ludicrous! The drunk man needs God to change him from the inside out. Then he'll be able to quit drinking because the reasons he started in the first place will no longer hurt.

So how do you, as the Scripture says, demolish strongholds in your life? How do you overcome an area that you have tried and tried to change with no success?

What you have to realize is, whether you want to be or not, you're in a war. The question is, are you getting stomped on, or are you winning? Maybe you're not using the weapons God has for you. Maybe you didn't exactly know who your enemy was or who you were fighting. The Bible says two things about this war:

> 1. Our battle is not with other people, it's with evil powers. (Eph. 6:10).
> 2. Our weapons are not carnal, they are spiritual (2 Cor. 10:4).

So in this war you're not fighting against people and you don't use guns and swords. The Bible says you're fighting against "rulers, authorities, powers, and spiritual forces of evil in the heavenly realms" (Eph. 6:12).

The spiritual weapons you have available to you are found in Ephesians 6:14-17:

> Stand firm then, with the belt of truth buckled around your waist, with the breastplate of righteousness in place, and with your feet fitted with the readiness that comes from the gospel of peace. In addition to all this, take up the shield of faith, with which you can extinguish all the flaming arrows of the evil one. Take the helmet of salvation and the *sword* of the Spirit which is the *Word of God.*

The amazing thing about the weapons God gives you is that only one is offensive. Every other weapon is used to defend yourself against Satan's attacks. But look at what God gives you to destroy the enemy: the sword of the Spirit which is the *Word of God.* That is the key to defeating the devil; using the Word of God against him.

When Jesus was tempted in the wilderness, He didn't have a wrestling match with the devil to defeat him. He didn't beg him to go away. He didn't just ignore him. He used the Word of God to resist him every time. If this was the way the *Son of God* overcame Satan, it is our example, also.

Change Your Mind

This war or battle you fight does not take place in the Middle East, nor does it take place against those who've mistreated you. It is within your mind that Satan darts his fiery arrows. If he can convince you of his ideas, he's won you over. Romans 1:12 says, "Do not conform any longer to this world [Satan's ideas] but be *transformed* by the renewing of your mind." In other words, if you want to get rid of the junk in your life, such as bad habits, bad thoughts, sin etc., you've got to get a new mind. You have to re-program your mind.

Your mind is just like a computer. You are the culmination of all of the data you've received over the years. Every rejection, every hurt, every cruel word has been programmed into your mind and you have either chosen to believe those words or reject them. Whatever your choices have been over the years programs your self-worth or self-esteem.

Another friend of mine, Mary Margarette, shares how she "changed her mind" and received her healing.

After a year and a half of struggling off and on, trying to be very secretive and hiding the binging and purging, my close friends and family began finding out. An eating disorder's closest friend is secrecy. When I began to realize how hard I was fighting and how much energy I was putting into keeping this monster hidden, I was shocked. I felt terribly guilty. All the emotions I had tried so long to push down and deaden started to rise up. I never before this felt bad about throwing up. I knew in my

81

head it was wrong, in the eyes of society and in the eyes of God, but my heart was in the dark.

When people started really confronting me about it, the light was turned on and the darkness was slowly being exposed. I was desperate. I could not live this way any longer. I began learning Scriptures that I never knew were in the Bible. The whole view I had of myself was opposite of the way God viewed me. I had to *throw everything I used to judge myself by society's standards out the window*. You never know you are living a lie until you know the truth!

Do you care more about looking like a girl in a magazine, or pleasing the Maker of heaven and earth? Who knows you better? Who loves you more? Who is wiser and truer? This world chewed you up and spit you out. But God says that you're fearfully and wonderfully made. He said that you're His child and you're precious and valuable to Him. I'd rather believe God!

I've read different materials that indicate that a majority of the models we see in magazines are anorexic. So when we compare our weight to those women, we are trying to achieve a standard that is not only unhealthy physically, but mentally, emotionally, and spiritually. Our country is in pretty sad shape if we equate beauty with sickliness.

Many young girls compare their own looks with different models or actresses and become frustrated when they can't have the same perfection. The truth is, those models don't really look as good as their pictures! Sure, there are pretty girls in the world, but no one looks perfect all the time. Yet we compare ourselves with pictures that they took hundreds of shots to get, airbrushed their skin to make it smooth-looking, put a fan in front of their face to blow their hair just the right way, and they spent seven hours on make-up and wardrobe in the first place! Who wants to spend that much time on themselves in the morning?!

The information that has formed the way we view ourselves is really based on a faulty set of values. In other words, it's a bunch of lies the devil has fed us all our lives to keep us from living the abundant life that God has for every one of us.

The truth is only found in the Word of God. You may say, "But it's *true,* I'm ugly, or I really can't do anything worthwhile." You need to begin re-programming your mind to believe what *God* says is true and not anyone else's opinion — not even your own.

God has a whole book packed with love notes to you that you've been ignoring, otherwise you wouldn't feel the way you do about yourself. He wants you to understand how valuable and how beautiful you are to Him so that you can become whole and love yourself, the way He loves you.

The same way you re-program a computer, by entering the proper data, you can actually change your thinking about yourself by meditating, memorizing, and speaking God's Word over yourself until you believe God's truth over the lies of rejection and pain from the past.

As I began to replace the negative thoughts about myself with the powerful Word of God, an incredible metamorphosis took place. I didn't stop binging and purging right away, but I began to love myself and think of myself the way God did. I knew I was free and that it would only be a matter of time before I would be able to stop overeating. Once I had been healed on the inside, the outward manifestation soon followed.

Recovery Workbook: Lesson 5
Live It Out!

Speaking God's Word is such an easy thing to do that many people think it's too elementary and never believe it would make a difference. In the following chapters you will gain more understanding of *why* you must speak it and not just think it. Also you will gain a new respect for the Bible and a desire to understand it. I will give you many more Scriptures to meditate on, but here are a few to begin with.

Remember, if God says it about you, you can say it about yourself. As you re-program your mind to think the way God does, you will know the truth and the truth will set you free (John 8:32).

If your mind says:

"I'm ugly," say *out loud,* "NO! I'm beautiful! I'm fearfully and wonderfully made!" (Ps. 139:13-16).

"I'm stupid" — "NO, I have the mind of Christ!" (1 Cor. 2:16).

"I can't!" — "No! I can do all things through Christ who strengthens me!" (Phil. 4:13).

"I'm fat" — "No! I'm made in God's image!" (Gen. 1:26).

"I'm weak" — "No! I'm strong!" (Joel 3:10).

We find freedom
when we find God;
we lose it when we lose Him.

PAUL E. SCHERER

Chapter 7

The Mystery of God's Word

God Created the World with a WORD

Genesis 1:1: "In the beginning God created the heavens and the earth" with His *words*. Verse 3: And God *said*, "Let there be light." Verse 6: And God *said*, "Let there be an expanse between the waters." Verse 9: And God *said*, "Let the water under the sky be gathered to one place." And so it goes on in verse 11, 14, 22, 24, and finally in 26: "Let us make man in our own image and likeness."

God actually created the heavens and earth with *words*. That's all — just words. Do you know anyone that can do that? The difference is, it was *God* who spoke those words. Think about that. God is so full of truth and integrity that when He speaks, it happens. Have you ever known someone you considered a person of integrity? You can always count on their *word*. They do not lie. It is even more so with God. He never lies and His word is the ultimate truth.

Now, let's stop a moment and think about the *Word of God*. What does that really mean? We hear the phrase as Christians so often that it obscures the truth and power behind it.

First of all, my definition of "word" means an exposed thought. So logically, the Word of God is the *thoughts* of God. How absolutely profound. Have you ever wanted to know what God was thinking or what's important to God? Have you ever wanted to know God better? You don't have to sit in solitude on the top of a mountain somewhere for days to find out! The answer is sitting on your shelf. (Hopefully not too dusty!) Read the *Bible!!* It contains the thoughts, purposes, plans, dreams, and desires of the Almighty God.

How to put the Word of God into Effect (Meditation)

The Bible is among the most respected and widely read books in this country. It's renowned for its literary accomplishments, its history, and its beautiful prose. Yet many people, from non-Christian scholars to Christians alike, can read the Bible and get absolutely nothing out of it. How can this be when the same power that created the heavens and earth lies within its pages? It takes more than just reading or even studying the Bible to tap into the power and blessings of God.

First of all, the Bible is not just another history book. We should have an awesome respect when we open its pages. It is the most powerful book in the world because it is *alive*.

For the word of God is living and active. Sharper than any double-edged sword, it penetrates even to dividing soul and spirit, joints and marrow; it judges the thoughts and attitudes of the heart (Heb. 4:12).

Libraries are full of literature containing man's philosophies and ideas. You could spend a lifetime learning worldly wisdom and not really be too much further ahead! Why not spend a lifetime studying, meditating, praying, and speaking God's Word? It will make you wise beyond your years, like David:

> Oh, how I love your Law! I meditate on it all day long. Your commands make me wiser than my enemies, for they are ever with me. I have more insight than all my teachers, for I meditate on your statutes. I have more understanding than the elders, for I obey your precepts (Ps. 119:97-100).

I was one of those Christians who read the Bible every day, yet I didn't have any power to change things. I *knew* a lot of its contents, but it didn't set me free from bulimia until I did a few things differently.

It takes meditation, memorization, and *application* for the power of God's Word to take effect in a person's life.

> Do not merely listen to the word, and so *deceive* yourselves. DO what it says. Anyone who listens to the word but does not do what it says is like a man who looks at his face in a mirror and, after looking at himself, goes away and immediately forgets what he looks like. But the man who looks *intently* into the perfect law that gives *freedom* and continues to do this, not forgetting what he has heard, but doing it — he will be blessed in what he does (James 1:22-25).

The Bible talks a lot about meditating on God's Word. We will gain great wisdom and spiritual understanding as we put it in our minds and think about it. Joshua 1:8 says, "Do not let this Book of the Law depart from your mouth; meditate on it day and night, so that you may be careful to do everything written in it. Then you will be prosperous and successful." Isn't that what the whole world is looking for?

Now, if Scripture is on our *mind* "day and night" as we meditate, then it stands to reason that it will begin to come out of our *mouths* as words, because a word is an exposed thought. So we will think God's Word, speak God's Word, and begin to act God's Word. If you think and talk about something long enough, you will begin to believe it and do it!

Remember the process of sin: thought, desire, attitude, action, and habit. It is also the process of a renewed or transformed mind. The only way to change bad thought processes, bad habits, and bad desires is to start at the thought level: meditation on God's Word. Then thoughts become words: speaking God's Word. Then words become action: doing God's Word.

The Power of the Spoken Word

Because we are made in God's image, and His Words are powerful, our words are also very powerful. Listen to what the Scripture says about the power of *our* words:

> The tongue also is a fire, a world of evil among the parts of the body. It corrupts the whole person, sets the *whole course* of his life on fire and is itself set on fire by hell (James 3:6).
>
> The tongue has the power of *life* and *death*

and those who love it will eat of its fruit (Prov. 18:21).

But the mouth of the fool invites ruin (Prov. 10:14).

He who guards his mouth and his tongue keeps himself from calamity (Prov. 21:23).

Your words have the power to direct the whole course of your life. Do you complain a lot and then when bad things happen say, "I knew that would happen — Didn't I say. . . ." This is the principle in action. The opposite is also true. If you speak life and blessing over yourself and your circumstances, you will see God's hand at work in everything you do. It will not be just positive thoughts or your own power that changes things, but God's Word. His truth will begin to destroy the work of the enemy in your life.

People often ask me," So, how did you get over bulimia?" It's a hard question to answer in just five minutes. I suppose that is why I wrote a whole book on the subject! But the bottom line, the simple truth is this: meditation and speaking God's Word out loud over and over until I absolutely believed its truths above everything else. That's what changed my thinking and my habits. I couldn't do it myself; I proved that over five years of my life. It was the secret of God's Word that did the work. And it still keeps changing me. I speak it over myself, my husband, our children, and our ministry. It changes hearts and lives, circumstances and destinies. The powerful Word of God brought forth the entire universe, and it is the very power that sustains our lives today.

So is my Word that goes out from my

mouth; It will not return to me empty, but will accomplish the purpose for which I sent it (Isa. 55:11).

Recovery Workbook: Lesson 6
Live It Out!

You may think, where do I start? The Bible is a BIG book and I don't know much. I suggest you take your prayer journal and begin by writing out Scripture on one sheet according to the topic. Eventually you can make sections of topics as your study increases. Some of my topics include, "I am valuable to God," "The power of the tongue," "Godly wife," "Children," "I am strong," "Overcoming sin," "Authority over Satan," "I have no fear," and the list goes on.

I found that the easiest way to study the Bible is by topics. Whatever you're interested in studying, write down as many Scriptures as you can find on the subject. Start in the topical index located in the back of your Bible. You may start out with topics such as "God loves me," "Forgiveness," "Positive things God says about me," and "Overcoming fear." Then begin speaking the Scripture over yourself in first person, in other words, writing, "God has not given *me* a spirit of fear," instead of *you* a spirit of fear, to make it personal.

I want to give you some Scripture that I started with which were the core verses that changed my life and helped me overcome bulimia and build my self-esteem. If you struggle with eating disorders or your self-esteem just needs a boost, start out with these. I also want to encourage you to *keep doing it* no matter if you feel a change or not. It took time to get the way you are, it also takes *time* to renew your thinking. Be patient and trust God! Happy studying!!

You are Valuable to God Scriptures:

Genesis 1:27	Isaiah 43:4
Zephaniah 3:17	Acts 10:15
Deuteronomy 33:12	1 John 3:1
Genesis 1:31	Isaiah 49:16
Psalm 139:13-16	Habakkuk 3:19

Colossians and Ephesians are also full of "who you are in Christ" Scriptures.

Scriptures on "speaking and meditating on the Word":

Joshua 1:7-8	Romans 12:2
Matthew 12:36-37	Deuteronomy 6:5-9
Isaiah 55:11	Romans 8:5-8
Hosea 4:6 11	Corinthians 10:4-5
Psalm 119:92	Psalm 119:97-104
Matthew 21:23	Hebrews 4:12

The greater the difficulty,
the greater the glory.

CICERO (106–43 B.C.)

Chapter 8

Kicking the Habit of Overeating

Fourth Step to Recovery

Stop! Before you read this chapter, if you have not read and applied the previous chapters, DON'T READ ON! These principles won't work until you know you are different and you *know* you really love yourself. Then you are ready to begin concentrating on how to stop the *habit*, or outside manifestation of the ED (eating disorder). If your self-image has not changed yet as a result of speaking God's Word over yourself, keep it up! It *will* happen, it just takes time. Remember, God's Word will not return to Him void. Then come back to this chapter when you've been transformed. Otherwise you won't have the power to deal with the habit part of the disorder and you will become frustrated. God always works from the *inside out.*

In recent years, I have experienced the same physical feelings of an ED when I have fasted. When you fast, your body gets extremely hungry and screams out in rebellion to get its needs met.

Fasting is an excellent spiritual discipline to teach us to "beat our bodies into subjection and make it our slaves" (1 Cor. 9:27). However, I recommend that persons struggling with ED's wait until they've completely recovered before they try fasting.

Ironically, bulimics experience the feeling of starvation almost daily. Michelle, writes about her feelings before and after a binge:

> Before a binge, I feel absolutely crazy! Binges would occur for me after a long period of starvation. My whole mindset was, "I can't eat." If I ate something "bad," I had blown it. I then felt completely out of control and would eat anything I had previously deprived myself of. My adrenaline skyrockets in this period and I relieve myself by purging, exercising, and taking laxatives. After purging, I'm completely satisfied, lacking emotion, relieved, released, warm, exhausted, and separated from what was bothering me before.

After a binge-purge cycle, or if you've starved yourself, you may feel ravenously hungry. Being so hungry makes you want to eat anything and everything. You fantasize about different foods, and when you finally get them, you gorge yourself. Then the fear and panic return. And so it begins again, purging, starving, and binging, a never-ending cycle that does not satisfy the real needs of the person.

During these surges, your body produces endorphins, or hormones, with tranquilizing and pain-killing capabilities that are secreted by the brain. This hormone is the same chemical released when you run long distances and is as addictive as opium. It gives you a high. No wonder so many young ladies with painful family backgrounds develop eating disorders.

The feeling of starvation is a panicky, shaky, almost delirious feeling, and urgent need for food. It creates headaches, stomachaches, drowsiness, and even blackouts. This is an everyday occurrence for both bulimics and anorexics. It's understandable why the binge/purge or binge/starve cycle exists. When a person feels the incredible urge for food because there is nothing in their stomach to sustain them, they can have an almost animalistic or insatiable craving to meet that need. With normal eating habits, this rarely if ever occurs because a person eating healthily will only feel mild hunger pangs when mealtime comes along. They eat a sandwich, meet the need, and forget about food until they get hungry again.

The Habit

If you have been involved in an eating disorder or some other unhealthy practice for a substantial amount of time, a habit has probably developed in your life. A habit is simply a practice that your body gets used to performing without much extra energy to propagate it. You may have already destroyed the spiritual stronghold which caused degrading thoughts in your mind and you can already tell a difference in your self-esteem, but now you must deal with the natural realm — the habit.

To me, the most difficult part of overcoming an eating disorder is the inside transformation. Once a person knows that God adores them and thinks they're awesome, no matter how they look, normal eating habits come much easier. The person who previously would do anything to themselves to get a certain "look," such as take pills, starve themselves, purge, now has a new-found respect for their body and will naturally nurture and take care of themselves.

When I first got a revelation of how much God loved me and that my body was a gift from Him, I couldn't bear to think of hurting it any longer. I would never do the things I had done to my own body to another human being, why would I do it to myself? I began to want to feed it healthy foods, get lots of rest, and get it back into shape. I finally loved myself.

It's just like your performance in school. If you have very loving, affirming parents, you are much more likely to get good grades than a student who has unloving, demanding parents. With a supportive "team" cheering you on, your self-esteem is higher and there is no tension or harsh pressure.

Likewise with weight. If you already know you're loved, there is no need to perform to gain acceptance; you're already accepted. If you hate yourself, it's very difficult to do anything productive.

We humans are very habitual creatures and sometimes it takes a bit of concentrated effort to change a deepseated habit such as our eating.

To begin to change the cycle of binging and purging, we must first understand the basic function of eating. This sounds ridiculous to someone who eats normally, but to the person with an ED, eating is a whole way of life. Bulimics love to eat. Anorexics love to avoid eating. God intended us to eat to live. He created a wonderful variety of foods for us to enjoy, but the whole purpose of food is to fuel our body so that we can function properly. Satan can take anything that God meant for our benefit and pervert it.

Obviously, we have to eat to live. Unlike alcoholics who must stop drinking cold turkey, bulimics cannot stop eating! The cycle of binge/purge must be stopped at the *binge level*, eating only as much as is needed to live a healthy life. (Many of these principles will work for undereaters as well, although they are directed more specifically to those who binge.)

Anorexics, on the other hand, must slowly begin increasing their caloric intake, knowing that God has created food and it is good.

Eating in moderation is of course relative, according to the particular person. It would be impossible to write out a set of rules that apply to everyone, but the concept of moderation is very scriptural:

> When you sit to dine with a ruler, note well what is before you and put a knife to your throat if you are given to gluttony. Do not crave his delicacies for that food is deceptive (Prov. 23:1-3).

"Look well" at the food in front of you and know that it is enough, you don't *need* more. Especially watch out for good-tasting delicacies; they deceive you into eating more than you should because they taste so good!

> If you find honey, *eat just enough*; too much of it and you will vomit (Prov. 25:16).

> Stolen water is sweet, *food eaten in secret* is delicious, but little do they know that the dead are there, that her guests are in the depths of the grave (Prov. 9:17-18).

The Scripture can't get any more blunt than that. God knows all about what we do in secret; He hates the things that destroy us and distract us from Him. But as much as He hates our sin, He also has the answers to our deliverance because He wants us to be close to Him even more than we want to be close to Him. He is on our side!

101

Are You Full Yet?

Your body was created to tell you when it is full. God put a "full-mechanism" inside your brain to tell you when to stop eating. It's natural to want to stop eating when you're full.

> He who is full *loathes* honey, but to the hungry even what is bitter tastes sweet (Prov. 27:7).

If you are overweight or bulimic, you have ignored that full-mechanism, and you must learn to listen to it again. Likewise, if you are anorexic, you have ignored your hunger mechanism. If God created our bodies to function in this way, then it only makes sense that it is *God's will* that we eat until we are full.

When I first started applying this principle, it took a lot of dedication and concentration. I was so used to *not* thinking whenever I was eating, I just crammed as much food down as fast as I could. I went far beyond my full-mechanism's beckoning every meal.

Eating until you're full is actually much more enjoyable, relaxing, and fulfilling than binging, and without all of the horrible consequences (such as feeling so full that you can't move, indigestion, guilt, vomiting, fear of getting fat, and the list goes on).

Before a meal I would sit down and think of all the consequences of my bulimic lifestyle, just to convince myself again that it really wasn't worth it to continue. Food has never satisfied anyone's deep needs of self-worth, fears, or feelings of being unloved. I would think of the agony and the guilt I always felt after purging, and wondering if I would get caught, or worse, the fact that God already knew what I was doing in secret. I would think of all of the money I had spent on endless fast-food restaurants and bags of groceries. It really wasn't worth all the lying that everything was okay, and that I was better now. How many times did I make "tomorrow's resolutions" to go on a diet or not to eat any more sweets. It really wasn't worth all the pain. Our ways reap destruction. But God's ways always reap blessing. Although eating only as much as you need is difficult at first, it doesn't compare with the pain of sin.

When you sit down to eat, first consider the consequences of *your* way. Then, consider what is before you. It is enough food. It's best to choose a healthy balance from the Four Basic Food Groups in the back of the book.

A word to undereaters: Some have ignored their "hunger call" so much that they can no longer distinguish how their stomach feels. They may eat a carrot and say, "I'm full." It may take a while to actually feel those hunger pangs again, but stay tuned to your body communication system and you will begin to recognize it. Eat whenever you are hungry, knowing that God has put that feeling there to tell you when your precious body needs fuel. In the meantime, you can use the proper (according to your height and bone structure) caloric intake of each food group as your gauge to tell you how much you should be eating. A good nutritionist would be able to help you plan a healthy, balanced diet that would give you all the nutrients you need without making you overweight. It also takes faith in God; knowing that as you obey Him by eating, that you can trust Him. He only has your best interests in mind and He wants you healthy, not overweight.

The next step, if you're an overeater, is to purpose in your heart to eat very slowly and carefully. Enjoy the flavor of each bite and enjoy your company. At first, it's best not to eat alone. It's so easy to fall again. Choose a friend who knows all about what you're going through and who won't judge you. Tell them about your commitment to eat only as much as you need.

Many times in college I would eat with Ron. I would be eating very slowly, concentrating on how I felt after every bite. The *second* I felt that full signal in my stomach, I'd take all the food in front of me, whether it was only half-eaten or three bites left, and shove it in front of Ron. Being a hungry college guy, he could eat all of his and mine too, to keep me from overeating!

I was very legalistic in obeying my full signals until I felt I had a handle on my eating. You have to re-learn to eat.

Now, I must warn you that everything within you will scream out in rebellion of your new-found eating habits. Oh, how our body hates discipline! You might cry or get angry. You are literally beating your body into submission and making it your slave instead of you being a slave to your body (1 Cor. 9:27).

Remember that even though it is painful now, God promises that it will produce a harvest of righteousness and peace (Heb. 12:11). That means victory is on its way!

KNOW THIS: The agony, anger, and pain that you may feel inside from giving up your need and craving for more food will *soon* pass. Hang in there! Pretty soon, you won't feel such a need to eat more. The more victories you get behind you, the less your body will rebel. Wait patiently upon the Lord. He will meet your need — the need that originally started this whole struggle, whatever it is — insecurity, fear, low self-esteem, self-hatred. "My God shall supply all your *needs,* according to His riches in Christ Jesus" (Phil. 4:19).

No temptation has seized you except what is common to man. And God is Faithful; he will not let you be tempted beyond what you can bear. But when you are tempted, he will provide a way out so that you can stand up under it (1 Cor. 10:13).

Wait for God to provide the escape. I remember countless times when I felt like I was going to scream, I was so frustrated. I was ready to blow my whole commitment, go out and eat everything in sight. And then I remembered the promise that God would make that way of escape. I'd pray through my tears, "God, I'm waiting . . . help me to be faithful to You!" And guess what, *God* was faithful. When we wait on Him, he always comes through for us. At every point of desperation, there would either be an encouraging friend who would walk by, a phone call, a Scripture that would give freedom or just plain Holy Ghost strength.

Sometimes I did fall. But I stayed with it and didn't let myself get discouraged. An athlete who misses the ball and then thinks about it will continue to make mistakes. In order to succeed he has to immediately forget his mistakes and go on. Pretty soon you will have more victories than defeats until you're 100 percent.

People can meet superficial
needs. But only God can meet
our deep needs.

FORRESTER BARRINGTON

Chapter 9

How to Eat

God has truly taken one of the greatest weaknesses in my life and made it a strength. I no longer struggle with weight or eating habits. I really have to give all the credit to God for this miracle. Even the practical principles on eating in this book are biblically based. You may find a different method of eating that you feel comfortable with, and that's great! As long as it's healthy, use it!

I came up with my methods of eating by researching Scripture and by questioning healthy, slim people. I simply asked them, "How do you eat?" The amazing thing that I observed was that they all seemed to eat anything they wanted, including sweets and other fattening foods, and still avoided gaining weight. Then I've known others who have dieted all their lives and never seem to lose weight, or if they do, they can't keep it off. How can that be? Thin people know some secrets that we're about to look at!

Most people, when they diet, deprive themselves of foods they really enjoy. Then later they often binge on the very thing they were depriving themselves of. They may see that piece of chocolate cake and say to themselves,

"I can't have that, I'm on a diet!" So, they go eat an apple, a box of crackers, some cheese and chips (now they've already eaten more calories than the cake), and then they say, "Oh well, I've already blown it, I'll just eat the cake, too."

See what happens? If they would have just eaten the cake in the first place, they would have saved a lot of calories. The secret is to eat all the fattening foods in smaller helpings, but don't deprive yourself.

If you want lasagna, eat a piece; not a huge piece, but eat it with a healthy salad. Then you'll be satisfied. Eat one piece of dessert, not two. Remember the commitment to eat only until you're full. If you're eating something you really love, and you find yourself getting full in the middle of it, ask for a doggy bag. Take it home and enjoy it later when you're hungry again. Then you'll get to enjoy it twice instead of pigging-out and feeling guilty!

I see people all the time trying to diet by cutting out meals. They think that if they only eat one meal a day, they're sure to lose weight. What they don't realize is, they are actually *lowering* their metabolism and making it harder for their body to ever lose weight.

The principle is this: Your metabolism is just like a fire. If you try to load a whole pile of logs on the fire at once, it will put the fire out. But if you continue to feed the fire smaller loads of logs, it will make the fire strong and hot.

The best way to raise your metabolism so that you can eat more food without gaining weight, is by eating more often and in smaller portions.

This is how thin people get away with eating whatever they want and still stay thin.

What to Do if You Overeat

I remember another commitment I made while on

my way to recovery. "Plan A" was to always eat only what I needed. "Plan B" was if I did mess up and binge, I could not purge, no matter what. You will find that binging without some way of getting rid of the food unnaturally is very undesirable. Some bulimics use laxatives instead of purging, but this is also very dangerous for the body and is considered a bulimic symptom.

The more you stick to your commitment to eat only what you need, the better you'll feel. If you do happen to overeat on occasion, don't worry. The horrible feeling of being too full *will* go away after a few hours. Just don't eat again until you're hungry. Having to pay the consequences of overeating is good for you, rather than purging and starting the whole cycle over again.

Even thin people overeat on occasion. There are times in our lives that a little overeating is okay — Christmas, Thanksgiving, happy reunions with family — as long as we don't do it meal after meal. Your body can handle a lot more food than you think. After overeating, we naturally feel that we have gained five pounds from one meal, but let me tell you, you won't! If you will wait until you're hungry to eat again, only eating a small meal or drinking juices following the meal where you overate, your body will compensate and you will not gain.

One last principle: Always check your motives when you are about to eat something. Are you truly hungry? *Never,* never eat when you are not hungry. If you're not hungry and you want to eat, you are again trying to fill an empty spot inside (not your stomach!) with food. And food will not satisfy it. People eat for all kinds of reasons; They're bored, lonely, depressed, fearful, stressed, etc. Go back to your Scriptures and feast at God's table. Then your heart will be filled to overflowing and your body will become healthy, fit, and trim!

THE PURSUIT OF BEAUTY

How sweet are your words to my taste,
sweeter than honey to my mouth! (Ps. 119:103).

Recovery Workbook: Lesson 7
Live It Out!

I want to remind you, even as you're working on your eating habits and the outward changes, keep growing inwardly by renewing your mind in Scripture. The self-control you have probably been experiencing is sweet indeed, but watch your back. The enemy can make you stumble very easily where you begin doubting yourself again and you must guard yourself wisely. "So, if you think you are standing firm be careful that you don't fall!" (1 Cor. 10:12). You will be protected within the safe walls of the Word. Twelve years later I *still* pray the Scriptures over myself. Self-esteem is one of the enemy's greatest attack zones!

All I do ought to be founded
on a perfect oneness with God,
not a self-willed determination
to be godly.

OSWALD CHAMBERS (1874–1917)

Chapter 10

Girls Aren't the Only Ones

Several years ago I was asked to speak for a particular eating disorder support group. As I walked in the room to survey the audience, I was very surprised to see two boys sitting in the group on either side of the room. My initial thought was that they were either accompanying a girlfriend, or had come to gain information to help someone else. As each person began to share their story, the two boys revealed they had eating disorders themselves. One had bulimia since pre-adolesence, the other, about 25 pounds underweight, had anorexia. They were just as desperate and frustrated as any girl in that room.

According to *Lifestyles* magazine, 10 percent of all patients treated for eating disorders are male, and it has been reported that as many as one million men may struggle with the diseases.

In school I knew of a guy who could put away an enormous amount of food. He would load up his plate with as many pancakes drenched in butter and syrup as he could stack, then inhale them, leave the room for a few minutes, and return to start all over again. We who knew him thought nothing of it at the time . . . he was a guy!

But later I found out the obvious truth: he was bulimic.

Eating disorders are generally much harder to recognize in males than females. 1. Overeating in males does not usually provoke as much attention as it does in females. 2. Males do not experience the loss of a menstrual period as females with eating disorders may. This would normally alert a physician of a problem. Therefore, a serious illness could take years to detect in a male unless there was great weight loss. 3. Many men are unaware that these diseases affect both sexes so they may fail to recognize the symptoms. 4. Men may shy away from admitting their disease or seeking medical attention for fear of being accused of having a "girl's disorder" or even a "gay-guy's" disease.

But the fact remains that the pressure to look good or fit is just as powerful for males as it is for females in our society. Why wouldn't they struggle with the same desperate compulsive behaviors to gain attention or acceptance?

Arnold E. Andersen, M.D., a professor of psychiatry at the University of Iowa College of Medicine spoke on his recent research of males with eating disorders:

> Males with eating disorders have been relatively ignored, neglected, or dismissed because of statistical infrequency or legislated out of existence by theoretical dogma. There's a need to improve our recognition of eating disorders in males and to provide more adequate treatment.
>
> We have to go back to where the roots are formed and look at gender diversity; for example, while women who develop eating disorders *feel* fat before they begin dieting, they

typically are near average weight, whereas the majority of men who develop the diseases actually are medically overweight. Males with eating disorders are also more likely than women to have alcohol-related conditions and obsessional features.

"More men who develop anorexia or bulimia were seriously teased as overweight children," Andersen said, adding that about 21 percent of males with eating disorders are gay.

Male Athletes and Eating Disorders

In certain sub-cultures of men, the pressure and competition is extremely fierce to look athletic and trim or be concerned about the fat content and muscle definition of the body.

Anderson says, "Males exposed to situations requiring weight loss — such as occurs with wrestlers, swimmers, runners, and jockeys — have a substantial increase in the behaviors of self-starvation and/or bulimic symptomatology follows, suggesting that behavioral reinforcement, not gender, is the crucial element."

A publication by the U.S. Food and Drug Administration titled *Conditions Men Get, Too,* by John Henkel, reports the following.

As a teenager, Gary Grahl was obsessed with having a trim, athletic body. The Wisconsin resident shunned food and exercised excessively. Sometimes he'd do situps and pushups for three hours before school. He ate little and shrank from 160 to an unhealthy 104 pounds. Over a six-year period he was hospitalized four times. Now 26, Grahl says he is "completely recovered" from his eating disorder.

An article titled "Lifestyles, the Overlooked Ten Percent," has the following to say about these health conditions which also plague boys and men:

> Neil Bardach remembers his experience on the wrestling team in high school. Even though he was never diagnosed with an eating disorder, he knows his eating habits were far from normal. Weighing 175 pounds today, he chose to wrestle at 130 pounds in high school. In season he would eat three to four meals a week. Although his coach talked of a healthy diet, he took it to an extreme to make weight, "looking at every ounce of liquid I put in my body." During one tournament he saw a wrestler collapse. The wrestler had taken a laxative to make weight, but because of fasting, his body had nothing to eliminate, and it just shut down.[6]

The "macho" image this society places on men to have lean, muscular, and athletic bodies is not what constitutes a real man according to God.

SECTION 3

TRUE BEAUTY

A healthy self-image is seeing
yourself as God sees you —
no more and no less.

JOSH MCDOWELL

Chapter 11

What is True Beauty?

I believe God has a standard of wholeness that He wants each person to attain. A whole person is a beautiful person, knowing who they are and able to reach out to others because of all God has done in their life.

This may be a hard saying to grasp, especially for younger women, but in the span of a whole lifetime, true beauty really does not come from the outside. The more a life is submitted to God, the more beautiful a person is.

Now I'm not saying we should throw out all our makeup and hair styles. We are God's representative on earth. If we can't relate to our own people, we'll never be able to win them over to our cause. We should respect ourselves and look like daughters of the King.

If we really love ourselves, we'll treat ourselves with respect. We'll begin accepting ourselves the way we were created. Some of us were built with a bigger bone structure. Others are naturally more slight. Some were born with curly hair, others with freckles. Don't always be trying to change or look like someone else! Just because a certain hairstyle is "in" doesn't necessarily mean it looks good on you. Wear it the way it looks best. Be yourself and celebrate the way God created you! If He truly knit you together in your mother's womb and made you with freckles, why are you trying to cover them up? If you've got curly hair, why are you always trying to straighten it? Be who God created you to be and don't constantly compare yourself with others.

Obviously, if you need braces or have a wart on the end of your nose, it's not wrong to correct the situation, but I'm trying to swing the pendulum the other way; to direct our attention to what God says is beautiful and on eternal things. This is where God says our beauty should come from:

> Your beauty should not come from outward adornment, such as braided hair and the wearing of gold jewelry and fine clothes. Instead, it should be that of your inner self, the *unfading* beauty of a gentle and quiet spirit, which is of great worth in God's sight (1 Pet. 3:3-4).

Our lives are made up of many different seasons. Just as there is a season for planting and a season for harvesting in the natural realm of life, so it is in the spiritual realm. When we're younger, natural beauty comes easy. I have two little girls. They delight my heart to look at them. They don't need make-up or hair spray to look presentable like I do! Their skin is like peaches and cream and their big bright eyes sparkle with life.

But our bodies begin to go through a natural process of deterioration when they reach a certain age. Our skin and hair gets dryer, our hands look aged. What we have planted in our younger years seems to show up or is harvested in later years.

You can see it on a person's face if they have had a

life of anger and bitterness. No amount of make-up will hide an ugly spirit. You can also see it if they have known and walked with the Lord for many years. Though they may have wrinkles and gray hair, their eyes sparkle. They have laugh lines on their face. Their spirit is full of life and joy. They've walked through good times and hard times with the Lord and they know His faithfulness. He shines through them and they are truly beautiful.

A clever piece from the book *The Velveteen Rabbit* by Margery Williams describes what I believe to be true beauty: A little stuffed rabbit is talking to an older, wiser toy in the nursery; the Skin Horse:

> "What is *REAL*?" asked the Rabbit one day, when they were lying side by side near the nursery fender, before Nana came to tidy the room. "Does it mean having things that buzz inside you and a stick-out handle?"
>
> "*Real* isn't how you how are made," said the Skin Horse. "It's a thing that happens to you. When a child loves you for a long, long time, not just to play with, but *really* loves you, then you become *Real*."
>
> "Does it hurt?" asked the Rabbit.
>
> "Sometimes," said the Skin Horse, for he was always truthful. "When you are *Real* you don't mind being hurt."
>
> "Does it happen all at once, like being wound up," he asked, "or bit by bit?"
>
> "It doesn't happen all at once," said the Skin Horse. "You become. It takes a long time. That's why it doesn't often happen to people who break easily, or have sharp edges, or who have to be carefully kept. Generally, by the time

you are *Real*, most of your hair has been loved off, and your eyes drop out and you get loose in the joints and very shabby. But these things don't matter at all, because once you are *Real* you can't be ugly, except to people who don't understand."

Recovery Workbook: Lesson 8
Live It Out!

You may need to do some practical things in order to really accept yourself. Again, this should be under the leading of the Holy Spirit. We're not trying to lay down another set of rules to follow. Pray and ask the Lord how you can begin to live out accepting yourself. I had to throw out all of my "glamour" and running magazines so that I'd stop comparing myself with others and the world's standard.

Write out anything that comes to mind for you to do in order to accept yourself:

_____
_____
_____

You may even have to start thanking God, out loud, for certain areas of your body or looks that you don't like. It is amazing how thanking God in "all things" builds a healthy appreciation.

I thank You, God, for exactly how You made me. Thank You for my:

_____
_____

In Luke 4:18-19 Jesus proclaimed His purpose and ministry in the temple when He quoted Isaiah 61:1-3. Read the passage in your Bible.

Now, make this true confession over yourself out loud!

> Jesus has bound up my broken heart. He's freed me and released me from darkness. He comforts me, provides for me, and bestows on me a crown of beauty instead of ashes, the oil of gladness instead of mourning, and a garment of praise instead of a spirit of despair!
>
> Believe it!

Keep your face to the sunshine and
you cannot see the shadow.

HELEN ADAMS KELLER (1880–1968)

Chapter 12

Your Purpose, Plan, and Destiny

Be Loved, and Love

I have a vision for this next generation of young women of God to become *real.* To rise to God's standard of beauty. They would not be focused on what women of the world are focused on; a certain look or image to attract attention and affection. But they would be filled to the brim with God's acceptance, God's love, and God's confidence. Their attention would not be on themselves, but on a hurting and lost world that so desperately needs what they have.

Your life has a great purpose. My life has a purpose. In finding that purpose, we find fulfillment and the meaning of life.

After the Lord set me free from the bondage of bulimia, I not only had a newly found self-control over my eating habits and brand new self-esteem, but I also had an incredible desire to love and give to the world. Only a loved person can truly love.

In the past, the church has taught to love the Lord first, others second, and ourselves last. To many churches, self-love has been considered a worldly teaching. They lump self-love with selfishness, self-centeredness and pride.

The only problem is, loving yourself last doesn't work. Yes, we are to be a servant of all, but there are too many broken and beaten people out there trying to take care of other broken and beaten people.

"Self-love," without God, is a worldly teaching. But there is no love outside of God. God is love and love is God. True love is not wrong. Therefore, loving yourself with God's love is *right*. God teaches us to love and value ourselves. Matthew 22:37-39 says, "Love the Lord your God with *ALL* your heart, mind, soul, and strength and love your neighbor *AS* you love yourself." If you don't love yourself, then you won't be *able* to love others. If you treat yourself like an old rag, used and abused, the Bible says that's how you'll treat others, also.

In order to really love yourself, or anyone else, you need to know how much you are worth.

How much *are* you worth? One hundred dollars? One thousand dollars? Maybe a million dollars? You don't have the authority to put the price on your life because you are not your own maker. God is your maker and He put a price on you. And God has already paid for it in full. You are worth His Son's BLOOD. Jesus paid for your life when He died on the cross and *that's* how much you're worth. Whether we think a person is worth something has nothing to do with the truth. God has already put a value on each human being and we must see ourselves and others the way He does. That's simply the truth.

If you can understand your own preciousness to God, then you will see others as precious to God as well.

These three loves are so interconnected that you can't separate one from the other. Love for God has to be first priority because He is the very essence of love.

The very reason God created mankind was to have someone to give himself to; someone to love. Have you ever wondered why you were created — why you are here? The soul purpose of your life is to be LOVED BY GOD. That's it! Nothing spiritual, He just wants to love you! He wants to reveal himself to you daily, and walk this life together, hand in hand. What an awesome God we have!

The nature of love is that it has to give — it cannot keep to itself or it wouldn't be love. Everything God has ever done, He did with us in mind, from the creation of the world to the redemptive plan. He thinks of us eternally. Hebrews 2:6-7 says,

> What is man that you are mindful of him,
> the Son of man that you care for him? You made
> him a little lower that the angels; you crowned
> him with glory and honor and put everything
> under his feet.

And He is still thinking of us — mankind — and how He can draw the world to himself.

When we really get a revelation of how much God loves us, something happens to us on the inside. We can no longer live for ourselves, thinking only of *"me."* God so loved the world that He *gave*. Since we're His kids and made in His image, we're like Him. So when we've got the same love He has inside, that can't stand alone, we have to *give*, too. We can't help it. It just keeps spilling out all over everyone around us! We start seeing the world like He does, and we have something to give them.

We have His compassion, His answers!

And when we've been healed of a wounded self-image, we're not always thinking of ourselves and how we can *get* love and acceptance from everyone else. We're not needy and insecure. We've got a full emotional cup, available to pour out on this needy world. It's amazing how a person's thoughts are much more directed towards *others* when they truly love themselves. God's ways are opposite of the world's ways.

I can honestly say that I am glad for the hard times I've been through. Surprisingly enough, I'm glad I had bulimia. Of course, if I could relive my life knowing what I know now, I'd never make the same wrong choices. But it is through the darkest times that I've had the greatest encounters with God of my life. I never would have learned to rely so deeply upon His Word. And I would never have known how much people suffer. I can empathize because I've been there.

After I was set free, I couldn't keep it to myself. I saw girls all over campus at my school struggling with the same things I had, and I had to speak! I had to tell them. I was zealous for the things of God. The Lord began opening doors to speak to different groups and talk with girls one-on-one almost daily.

It was incredibly fulfilling to see others be set free using the same principles I used from Scripture. God's Word works for anyone who believes!

One word of caution before you go exploding all over everyone with your new-found profundity and wisdom. Be careful, especially if you've just been healed, not to get too cocky about your new strength. The Bible says that pride comes before a fall. Satan's mad enough that you've been delivered, let alone that you are helping others get set free, also. It is his plan to keep them in bondage for the rest of their lives. He will try to tempt you and make you fall again.

> So, if you think you are standing firm, be careful that you don't fall! No temptation has seized you except what is common to man And God is faithful; he will not let you be tempted beyond what you can bear (2 Cor. 10:12-13).

It happened to me several times before I realized what was happening. I was going along just great until I'd get asked to speak about my testimony. Then all of a sudden, I'd be tempted again, and sometimes I'd even fall. I finally told a friend of mine and we began to pray for protection and strength each time I'd go to minister. It made all the difference in the world. Give yourself a little time to just be normal and to live out your freedom before you help everyone else. Once you're strong and solid, let God turn you loose and see His power change some lives!

However mean your life is,
meet it and live it;
do not shun and call it hard names.
It is not so bad as you are.
It looks poorest when you are richest.
The faultfinder will find faults even
in Paradise. Love your life.

HENRY DAVID THOREAU (1817–1862)

Chapter 13

Consumed by the Call

Since my deliverance, I feel like my life has been in overdrive. Pre-deliverance days were long and painful, but once my life was in a place where God could use me, I was put in all kinds of leadership and speaking opportunities. God will use anyone who is willing and prepared.

I married Ron Luce, love of my life, which has been a whirlwind in itself! One year after we were married, we hit the mission field for eight months. I had never really experienced Third World countries firsthand before. I was in total shock! But what happened in those few months totally changed both Ron and me forever. It shaped our entire mindsets and changed our career plans. It became the life-blood, the very essence and motivation for why we live! I guess you could say, we found our purpose.

I had never cared about people of different ethnic backgrounds before, but God began to give me new eyes. We saw people who lived on dump heaps and in paper boxes. We saw children with flies all over their little bodies and swollen stomachs from malnutrition. We saw desperate looks in the faces of countless people who were hungry for truth. Everyone has seen those faces on TV, but it's different when those faces are looking at you. You can't switch the channel.

I can't describe to you how deeply those scenes affected me. If you've ever wondered if Christianity is really the only way — go! You'll never wonder again after you've seen the effects of Islam, Buddhism, Hinduism, and spiritism on an entire culture of people. Those religions don't give anyone a quality of life. They only bring bondage to religious rituals, poverty, and destruction.

During those eight months that Ron and I traveled and observed, we prayed for God's heart and direction for our lives. We were privileged to preach and bring the truth to thousands of hurting people. We "dined" with a family, sitting on the floor of a tiny thatched-roof house and ate rice off of banana leaves. We saw miracle after miracle everyday. The blind and the deaf were healed and God protected us in countless ways. It was the most exciting experience either of us had ever had.

We began thinking — if God could use US in these ways, He could use just about anybody! After much prayer and wise counsel, we decided to take teenagers overseas to experience God's heart and miracles for the world firsthand; and Teen Mania was birthed.

Beauty, unaccompanied by virtue,
is as a flower without perfume.

FRENCH PROVERB

Chapter 14

The Final Commission

I want to leave you with a few thoughts as you come to the end of this book.

The title and theme of the book is our own pursuit of beauty in ourselves. What does that really mean, and where can we find true beauty? I believe it's found in finding our *purpose* — whatever purpose God has created you for, and fulfilling it. Only you can find it. No one can tell you what you were destined to be.

I may not know what your purpose is specifically, but I do know what God wants to do in this world. God wants to take a generation of broken-hearted young people and transform them into world-changers for His glory. It is His glory because most of this generation is not strong to begin with. They desperately need God to make them *real* and *whole*.

As they become all they were created to be, they begin to look around and see a world full of people who are as broken as they were. But they also see and feel an incredible sense of love and compassion for these people that they've never felt before. In fact, it's so overwhelming that they can't just ignore it, or go on with their business as usual. They must act. They must do what they see their Father doing.

It is our conviction that "Go ye therefore into all the world" is not a suggestion, it is a command, for every Christian. It is also a very possible command. We tell people, "Just go on one short-term mission trip. You don't have to pack up and move away for 30 years to get the world in your heart." You don't have to change all of your career plans, but just *go once* and see what God will do.

There are those that cannot possibly go because of physical illness or various responsibilities, but they have a mouth and they can pray. They have a checkbook and they can send someone else! Everyone is called to play a part in fulfilling the Great Commission.

You may not be called to missions but rather called into the business world. Great! Take your vacation time just once, but go! God wants to give you a heart for the world just as much as He does a person in full-time ministry. After you have gone once, it will change your whole perspective on life. You may do business differently or have a more God-centered emphasis in your career. Whatever you were born to do can affect others here and around the world for His kingdom. Get a vision!

Some say, "Well, we need to concentrate on America. Your mission field is in your own back yard." I say, yes, we need to reach those who are here, but the truth is, if they really wanted to know about God, they could turn on the TV or radio to a Christian station, or walk down the street a couple of blocks to the nearest church. If they are really hungry there's plenty of spiritual food here in the States. We have stacks of different translations of the Word of God, the Bread of Life. But the little girl in India has never even tasted *one* slice. Is it fair?

The Lord says, "Who will go, who shall I send?" Let our hearts say, "Send *me* Lord!"

God has a purpose for you beyond your comprehension. His purpose will bring more satisfaction and fulfillment than you've ever known. Let Him heal you, restore you, and fill you with His ambitions.

Then, when you stand before Him in glory, He will say to you, "Well done, my good and faithful servant."

And you will have found true beauty.

SECTION 4

.

THE PREVENTION OF EATING DISORDERS
AND
HELPING THOSE WHO HAVE THEM

The best part of beauty is that which

no picture can express.

FRANCIS BACON (1561–1626)

Chapter 15

How to Help Someone with
an Eating Disorder

One of the most frequently asked questions I receive about eating disorders is "How can I help my friend or child deal with their eating disorder?" This is a difficult question, namely because the success of a person's life is ultimately up to that person, not another. We all tend to want to "fix" or manage other's lives, but God only gives us the power and authority to change our *own* lives. If we could just get our anorexic to eat more or our bulimic to eat less, then we'd have it made! As much as we desperately want them to be well, it won't happen until they are ready to make the necessary changes themselves. However, there are some things that we can do to help posture and motivate them to want to receive their healing.

As I have stated in numerous ways in the above chapters, your primary concern must be the inward condition of the person's heart, not the outward manifestations. It is difficult for us, especially dealing with something as bizarre as an eating disorder to avoid focusing on behavior, because that is what we can see.

Look at the person for who she is and avoid labeling her as "the bulimic" or "the anorexic." She may have deep wounds that God wants to heal. It is not a matter of her wanting to be more attractive, although that plays a small part. Her heart condition is showing up through her eating disorder. When her heart is healed and her self-esteem is intact, then she will be able to eat normally again.

If the person is deemed anorexic, her weight loss is drastic, and her health is in danger, she may need to see a doctor immediately. Hopefully, her condition will be detected before it is that critical. In most cases hospitalization is not necessary, and these are the cases that I would like to address.

The disorder must be confronted in complete acceptance and love. A person doesn't just "grow out of it" and it will only worsen unattended. Many of us are afraid of confrontation and hate to make waves. Don't avoid conflict, it could cost a precious life.

In dealing with someone with an eating disorder, always approach her in an unthreatening manner. Otherwise, she will immediately cut off all communication with you for fear of disapproval. Speak kindly, gently, and full of concern.

Here are some helpful hints:

1. Don't bring attention to weight, good or bad.

An obvious error would be, "You're looking a little chunky, Betty. You could stand to take off an extra 20." The opposite can be just as detrimental. Anorexics and bulimics thrive on comments such as, "You're looking great! Have you lost weight?" Although that kind of comment would be intended for encouragement, it would only serve to fuel the fire and motivate her to work harder to lose weight. The best encouragement would be to bring attention to her overall beauty, or better yet, her inner beauty or character.

2. Don't bring attention to different body parts, even in jest.

Fathers are famous for this. I can't tell you how many stories I've heard and read where a dad gave a comment in passing, "But I was only teasing! How could she have taken me seriously, she looks fine!" But it was that one little statement that she remembered, and in fact, triggered her whole eating disorder. Girls desperately need their father's approval and acceptance. No matter how they look, they need to know that they are still daddy's little princess. When they really feel secure in their father's love, they won't be looking for another prince to fill that gap in their heart. *Please,* parents, watch your words.

3. Accept her unconditionally.

Again, I write this primarily to parents. We all want our children to succeed. We want them to be better than we are. But do we have unrealistic expectations that are driving them to an unhealthy perfectionism? Ask yourself some hard questions such as:

a. Do I love _____ according to her performance?

b. Do I have unrealistic expectations of my child that drive her to strive for approval? (Such as grades, sports, other activities?)

c. Do I place too much emphasis on appearance?

d. Do I place too much emphasis on food?

4. Don't police her eating.

This is a hard one, especially when she lives under the same roof. When she feels that you are hanging over her shoulders, watching every bite, it will become tense in your household. If you force her to eat everything, she may even comply, but you can be sure that she'll excuse herself to the bathroom and exert her own will. It is a control issue. The answer, I believe, lies in helping her to know who she is in Christ and also good, solid nutrition.

5. Educate her in who she is in Christ.

This is, by far, the greatest thing you can do to help someone with an eating disorder. Her age will dictate how pro-active you are in helping her. Use the principles I've drawn out in this book and teach her. If she is more self-motivated and seems ready for answers, have her read it herself. But you can still encourage her by saying things like "Michelle, you are fearfully and wonderfully made! You are wonderful! God thinks so, and so do I!"

6. Educate her in good nutrition.

This may be an area that affects you as well, but all for the better! Sit down with her and learn the Four Basic Food Groups. Learn what each group does for the body and why we need things like proteins daily. Learn how many calories are appropriate for good health. It is amazing how inept most of us are when it comes to basic nutrition. We can eat a myriad of healthy foods, raise our metabolism, and keep a steady weight with a lot less effort than those with eating disorders exert. It is God's way of fighting obesity and many, many diseases.

7. Communicate!

a. Communication starts with listening. Do you really listen to your child? Do you look in her eyes and hear her heart, or are you thinking about what you're going to say next?

b. When you speak, do you share your heart, or is it always on a surface level? People need to love and be loved *deeply*. That's what families are for!

c. *How* do you communicate? With screaming, or self-control? With constant correction, or with more encouragement? With harsh or kind words?

These issues touch us all to the core, but they have everything to do with someone who is struggling with an eating disorder. We must search our own hearts, evaluate our lives, and see how we can love and live more like Jesus. This will produce an atmosphere of real healing for "the wounded."

8. Pray, pray, pray!

It has been said, "All we can do now is pray!" Whoever said that didn't understand what prayer is all about — hooking up with the Most High God! He is the only one who can change hearts and lives. "The prayer of the righteous avails much."

I want to encourage you, especially the parents of someone with an eating disorder. Watching your child's misery is heart-wrenching, I know — I put my own mother through much grief. But your child is God's child, and He loves her even more than you do. Don't ever give up. You will see the fruits of your labor.

> Jesus replied, "I tell you the truth, if you have faith and do not doubt, not only can you do what was done to the fig tree, but also you can say to this mountain, 'Go, throw yourself into the sea,' and it will be done. If you believe, you will receive whatever you ask for in prayer" (Matt. 21:21-22).

A Word to Parents on Prevention

Prevention goes hand in hand with the principles we have already discussed in the previous chapter, but I wanted to address parents on the issue of our responsibility towards our children who have not yet experienced the heartaches of eating disorders.

This age is a sight and sound generation. Image and power is everything. We have veered far from God's biblical standards, and the young ladies with eating disorders are paying for it dearly.

It is our responsibility as parents to instill God's principles in their hearts while they are still young. The Bible directly instructs us:

> Train a child in the way he should go, and when he is old he will not turn from it (Prov. 22:6).

> These commandments that I give you today are to be upon your hearts. Impress them on your children. Talk about them when you sit at home and when you walk along the road, when you lie down and when you get up. Tie them as symbols on your hands and bind them on your foreheads. Write them on the doorframes of your houses and on your gates (Deut. 6:6-9).

In other words, *WE* must train our children in the ways of God *everywhere, all the time*, and then we can be assured of them always following after Him.

What does the Bible say about image and appearances? God's viewpoint is very much opposite to this world's.

> But the Lord said to Samuel, "Do not consider his appearance or his height, for I have rejected him. The Lord does not look at the

things man looks at. Man looks at the outward appearance, but the Lord looks at the *heart* (1 Sam. 16:7).

KATIE LUCE

What a rich heritage we could give the young people of this coming generation to be more concerned about their own and other's hearts, rather than outward appearances. But we must first make sure that we've adopted God's priorities as our own. It only stands to reason that if we ourselves are caught up in appearances, then we will naturally transfer those values into our children.

Real Christianity is adopting God's values and principles for every aspect of life, not just going to church on Sunday and paying our tithes. It calls for:

1. Putting Jesus Christ at the helm of our lives in every area and living biblical standards.

2. Loving and nurturing our spouses and honoring the divine institution of marriage as the highest priority under our relationship with God.

3. Placing the priority of family and children above our careers or financial and social status and pro-actively training our children in godliness.

If we will be obedient to God's Word, He promises that we will have good success and everything we put our hands to will prosper.

Let's not just give lip service to the King of kings. Let's honor Him by laying down our lives, taking up our crosses, and following Him. Then we will find real life.

Endnotes

[1]"Dying to be Thin," *Family Circle*, 2/23/88, vol. 3, p. 58-63.

[2]"Bulimia: A Woman's Terror," *People Weekly*, 11/17/86, vol. 26, no. 20, p. 36-41.

[3]*Sports Illustrated*, 8/8/94, vol. 81, no. 6, p. 52-60.

[4]John Goodbody, *Illustrated History of Gymnastics.*

[5]The following sources were used in Chapter 2:

Newsgroups: Alt. Support. Eating-disorders: Article 6011, Subject: Eating Disorders Frequently Asked Questions, I Diagnosis, July 13, 1995.

Diagnostic Criteria are from American Psychiatric Association Committee on Nomenclature and Statistics: Diagnostic and Statistical Manual of Mental Disorders, 3rd ed. rev. Washington DC, American Psychiatric Association, 1987.

Sources for definitions include: American Psychiatric Association Diagnostic and Statistical Manual of Mental Disorders D9m-IV. 4th ed. Washington, DC, 1994; *Food for Recovery,* by Joseph D. Beaseley and Susan Knightly, Crown, New York, 1994; Overeaters Anonymous. The Twelve Steps and Twelve Traditions of Overeaters Anonymous, Los Angeles, CA, 1993.

Definitions researched and edited by Jean S. and BJM, 9/94.

[6]"Lifestyles, the Overlooked Ten Percent," Nicole Maestri, Bucknellian staff writer, 4/18/96.